# LYNN SEYMOUR

*An Authorised Biography*
*Richard Austin*

Angus and Robertson Publishers

**Picture Credits**

Associated Television Ltd., p. 217, Ken Bell Photography Ltd., p. 159, Jane Bown, p. 120, Harry Cantlon, p. 25, Central Press Photos Ltd., p. 191, Anthony Crickmay, p. 207, Condé Nast Publications Ltd., p. 144, Zoe Dominic, pp. 82, 83, 98, 99, 104–105, 112, 185, Mike Humphrey p. 222, Keystone Press Agency Ltd., p. 103, Lara Ley, p. 88–89, Fraz Lindner, Photo, p. 87, MIRA, p. 182, Roy Round, p. 59, Houston Rogers Collection— Theatre Museum, London, p. 65, Leslie E. Spatt, pp. 129, 130–131, 154, 177, 181, 194, 196, 198, 201, 204, Trans-Canada Airlines, p. 29, Telegraf- Maschler, Berlin, p. 156, Jennie Walton, pp. 178, 186, 192, 200, Victor Welch, pp. 171, 175. The publishers are also indebted to Miss Lynn Seymour for the loan of pictures reproduced in the book.

ANGUS & ROBERTSON · PUBLISHERS
London · Sydney · Melbourne · Singapore ·Manila

First published in the United Kingdom by Angus & Robertson (UK) Ltd in 1980

First published in Australia by Angus & Robertson Publishers Australia in 1980

Copyright © Richard Austin 1980

ISBN 0 207 95900 5

Typeset by Computacomp (UK) Ltd, Fort William, Scotland

Printed in Hong Kong

*For Kenneth MacMillan*

## Previous Books by the same Author

I a woman with the taint of the pioneer in my blood
Full of youthful strength that wars with itself and is lawless ...

*Katherine Mansfield.*


If only one could tell true love from false love as one can tell
mushrooms from toadstools ...
It takes a dreadful number of toadstools to make you realize
that life is not one long mushroom.

*Katherine Mansfield —Journal.*


It is like a bullfight. Everyone is waiting for a bucket of blood
and if they don't get it they are disappointed. I think you
ought to let every vein.

*Lynn Seymour.*

# CONTENTS

# ACKNOWLEDGEMENTS

In the first instance I should like to express my gratitude to Dame Ninette de Valois DBE, who most kindly agreed to write the Foreword to this book despite a schedule that demanded a great deal of travelling and many engagements.

I owe a particular debt of gratitude to Miss Lynn Seymour's mother, Mrs Marjorie Springbett. Not only did she provide me with many hundreds of letters, written to her by her daughter over a period of fifteen years, but she went to the great trouble of cataloguing these in date order. In addition she provided me with innumerable press cuttings, photographs and personal reminiscences for which I am indebted. No one could have been more patient in answering my questions, or gone to more trouble to put me in contact with others.

I am very grateful to the following friends and colleagues of Miss Seymour who found the time in their very busy lives to talk to me and who also, in some instances, provided me with letters and photographs: Dame Ninette de Valois DBE, Sir Robert Helpmann CBE, Mr John Field CBE, Miss Winifred Edwards, Mr Christopher Gable, Mr Kenneth MacMillan, Mr Peter Wright, Mrs Jill Harris MBE, Mrs Lara Ley and Mrs Fay Angus.

My thanks are also due to Miss Myra Armstrong, Press Secretary of The American Ballet Theatre, who provided me with information about Miss Seymour's appearances with the Company. I am also grateful to Mr W. Paterson Ferns of Nielsen-Ferns International and Mr Tony Gruner of Talbot Television Ltd, who allowed me access to the television film, *Lynn Seymour: In a Class of her Own*, prior to its public screening. I must also thank Miss Daphne Probyn of the Canadian Broadcasting Corporation who obtained tapes of interviews given by Miss Seymour and broadcast by CBC, and also Miss Jenny Webb of the BBC for her research on programmes featuring Miss Seymour and televised on the BBC.

Miss Leslie Spatt gave me invaluable advice about photographs, as did Mr David Leonard of Dance Books Ltd, who also gave me his help most generously on other matters. A considerable amount of the factual background to this book was obtained from the magazines *Dance and Dancers* and *The Dancing Times* for the period from 1954 to 1979, although any errors in fact or omissions in detail are my entire responsibility. I am also most grateful to Miss Brigitta Arora who helped so much with picture research.

I should like to thank the many people in Canada who helped me with advice and information, including: Mrs Margaret Bruce, Mrs

Rosemary Deveson, Mrs Twyla Graeme, Mrs Vera Zabiak, Mrs Margaret Anne Lewis, Mrs Rose Hunter, Mrs Dora Marrion, Councillor Lilian Coade, Mr H. B. Smith, Mrs Buchanan and Mrs Consuelo Torey, Director of Ballet at the Vancouver YWCA.

Once again I must express my gratitude to Miss Mary Scudamore who assisted me in correcting the proofs. I should also like to thank Miss Audrey Coleman of London Weekend Television Ltd, Mr Barry Ledingham of ATV Network Ltd, Miss Francesca Frankie of the Friends of Covent Garden archives at the Royal Opera House, and Mrs Rebecca Read for her help over the various drafts of the original mss. I am most grateful to Mr Martin Lewis who most generously allowed me to study his personal scrapbook relating to Miss Seymour.

Even with the kindness and consideration of all those mentioned above, this book could never have been written but for the generous help given to me by its subject, Miss Lynn Seymour CBE, whose dancing was its first inspiration. Miss Seymour read through the entire manuscript, both in its first draft and in the final version, correcting a number of errors in fact and chronology, as well as amplifying many points on which I was in doubt. In doing this she showed me the rare consideration of never pressing me to alter an opinion, either on artistic or personal matters, even when she was not fully in accord with what I had written or had reservations about some of the conclusions I had drawn. This book is, I hope, some expression of my gratitude to her.

For permission to use copyright material, acknowledgements are made as follows: for quotations from *The Waste Land, Burnt Norton* and *Little Gidding* from *Collected Poems 1909–1962* by T. S. Eliot, to Faber & Faber Ltd; for the passages from *Camera Man* by John Gale, to Hodder & Stoughton Ltd; the selections from *Poems* by George Seferis reprinted by permission of The Bodley Head; for the quotation from *Le Blé en Herbe* by Colette to Librairie Ernest Flammarion; for the passage from *The Adventures of a Ballet Critic* by Richard Buckle to Hutchinson Publishing Group Ltd; for the quotation from *Selected Poems* by John Heath-Stubbs, to the author and Oxford University Press; for the quotation from *Robert Helpmann* by Elizabeth Salter to Angus & Robertson Publishers.

# Foreword

W E HAVE FOUND a lovely child in Canada.' Many years ago these words greeted me on the return of the Royal Ballet staff from a Canadian tour. Lynn Seymour was very youthful looking, a vulnerable and sensitive character who showed a charm that was allied to a great talent. I watched the progress with the alerted interest I had felt for Margot Fonteyn at about the same age. Her future seemed assured to me, coupled as it was with a natural spirit of adventure. There was also present a streak of independence and a largesse of personality that—as in all such cases—does more for others than for the individual concerned.

Kenneth MacMillan was quick to pick her out (when they were working together in the Sadler's Wells Royal Ballet group) as his choreographic muse for then and all the years to follow. They did a great deal for each other's careers. Such partnerships are as important as the legendary partnerships of certain great dancers.

Lynn Seymour will go down in the history of the first fifty years of the Royal Ballet as the greatest dramatic dancer of that era.

*Dame Ninette de Valois*

# PART ONE

# 1: *Childhood*

*I*T MUST HAVE BEEN the warmest day of summer. Now as it drew towards evening the heat had little abated. It shimmered over the city, and people began to think of the beach and the long, slow twilight which at this time of the year in Vancouver often brought a cool breeze blowing in from the sea. The rush hour had begun. Queues formed at the bus stops. The streets were noisy and congested; not a breath of wind stirred. Every great city in the world is like this in the early evening, with the same thirsty, hot and bad-tempered commuters waiting for buses or the delayed underground train.

Suddenly two small girls emerged from a side street, one balancing a tray of paper cups filled with lemonade, the other carrying a small folding table. They approached the queue, quietly triumphant. They were aged between eight and nine— one sturdily built, the other slighter, hair in a pony-tail and her mouth drawn in a determined line. She wore a tee-shirt, faded blue shorts and sandals. She had rather heavy shoulders and long legs, so that she appeared a little unbalanced with her tray of cups.

The children did a marvellous trade. All the lemonade was sold at the knock-down price of five cents a cup and before long replenishments were needed. With a quick reassuring word to those at the end of the queue, both girls dashed away down the street. The small one led, leaping and swerving between the crowds. She moved with a kind of careless, abandoned grace; indeed it was almost like a dance.

Lynn Springbett, later to be known in the world of the dance as Lynn Seymour, *prima ballerina*, was born in Wainwright,

Alberta, on 8th March 1939. As this child was one day to become a pioneer in her art, it is not surprising that her free and adventurous spirit was to be found in ancestors who came from the great prairies around the Rocky Mountains. Her great-grandfather on her mother's side, Robert McIvor, was of Scottish descent. The McIvors are members of the Campbell clan and in the sixteenth century were estate managers of Inverary Castle in Argyll. A cobbler by trade, Robert McIvor lived in a little town called Lion's Head, situated on a bay of Lake Huron in Ontario.

It was a close-knit little community, settled on the shores in this beautiful landscape; most earned their living either as fishermen or farmers. It was an ordered, simple life: a small, contented backwater in what was still a new land, where the spirit of the first pioneers was never far back in history and was recalled in many family tales. This is a great distance indeed from the cities and opera houses of the world in which Lynn was to discover her fame, for such splendours were unknown to them. They were content to spend the summer evenings bathing in the lake; in winter, skating on the ice that covered it for months on end. It was a quiet place to live. It is not surprising that her great-grandfather had no less than thirteen children.

One of these, Alexander McIvor, was Lynn's grandfather. He fell in love with a local girl, Bertha Lindsay, whose father was a fisherman on the lake. Often he would take Bertha out in her father's boat; the long summer days and evenings of their courtship were idyllic—the huge silence, the rippling water; around them the great curve of the bay and the wooded hills beyond. Alexander was the success of the family, graduating in chemistry at the University of Toronto and taking up the career of a pharmacist. After he married Bertha he settled in a small town near Winnipeg called Souris, where Lynn's mother was born.

In 1910 Alexander McIvor built a wing on to a general store owned by his brother in Cowley, situated in the wide ranching country near the Rocky Mountains, and set up his own pharmacy. It was a tiny place with no school and only a few wooden-built shops, straggling along the dusty main street towards the great prairie lands beyond. Lynn's mother, Marjorie, had to ride double with another girl on horseback to the nearest school over a mile away, whether in the blazing

12

heat of summer, when the dry winds blew suffocatingly across the plains, or in the blinding snows of winter, when teams of horses with jingling bells pulled farm waggons on sled runners and the blizzards swirled in the icy dark of evening. Much lighter sledges, known as 'cutters', carried up to three passengers with buffalo robes pulled over the knees and feet and hot bricks on the floor to keep their feet warm.

Later the family moved to the larger town of Calgary, where Alexander had his own store and there they lived until he retired. Marjorie loved the open life of Canada, as her daughter was to love it as well. She rode, swam, played tennis, baseball and basketball, and in the winter she and all her friends went skating. In 1922 she left home to take up a teaching post in Otenalta in south-east Alberta. There she met her future husband, Ed Springbett, who was the principal of a four-roomed school where Marjorie taught.

Ed's family had emigrated from England to Ontario; his father was a blacksmith who had married a Scottish girl, Christina McQueen. He was a true pioneer who founded Red Deer, the town that grew up around his forge over the years. Ed was a small, wiry, young man whose real ambition was to become a doctor, but as the family were poor and could not finance him through university, he took a teacher's training course when he was demobilised from the Canadian air force at the end of the First World War. He later decided to make a career in dentistry and began his studies at the University of Alberta in Edmonton. He and Marjorie married in 1928.

Then followed the years of the financial depression in Canada, during which Ed had to give up his studies for a time and return to teaching with his young wife. When he resumed them at the University, he was obliged to take many kinds of odd jobs during vacations so that they could survive; it was a terrible struggle to make ends meet. Their son Bruce was born in 1932 and shortly afterwards the family moved to Wainwright, a town east of Edmonton, where Ed set up a practice. Poverty and unemployment were so widespread that his patients often paid their bills in kind: it was not unusual for a farmer to leave a goose or a pair of chickens in payment for his treatment, as well as fruit or vegetables from his garden. It was here in Wainwright that the second child, Lynn, was born.

With the outbreak of war Ed enlisted in the Canadian

Dental Corps in 1941 and was sent to Victoria to train. Marjorie stayed behind to sell up the house and its contents and then with her two children travelled by car over a thousand miles to Vancouver, where Ed was now posted at Brigade Headquarters on Vancouver Island. It was desperately difficult to find anywhere to live; the city was overcrowded with service families from all over Canada. They stayed in rooms and rented flats both in Vancouver and Victoria. After Ed was demobilised he set up his practice again in Vancouver, and in 1947 his surgery was ready for use. At last they knew security: the years of hardship and continual disruption were at an end. They had a home at last—a flat near the beach. They had their two children and a future to build for them both.

In spite of the disruptions of those early war-time years, Lynn grew up as a lively, high-spirited child, restless, easily bored and very determined. This shows from the earliest photographs—the eyes looking straight into the camera, as though she challenged it. Even when very young she could, however, be dissuaded from a course of action by logical argument from her parents. She was not prepared to take things on trust or as commands from above; but she was the first to enjoy a good argument which must be tested, even disputed, before acceptance.

The only problem in her very early years was with her eyesight. Under stress or fatigue, one eye was inclined to turn inwards—a disability that still affects her today. Eye exercises were tried, then glasses; and before they settled in Vancouver she had three operations that she accepted with a calm stoicism, remarkable in a young child.

Lynn's mother was tolerant, highly patient and quick to encourage any sign of independence in her children. By nature warm-hearted, outgoing and generous, she provided an easy and relaxed background. Her father was quieter, more reserved; still a teacher at heart, he insisted that Lynn should learn something new every day which he explained to her with the use of a small blackboard.

Her brother, seven years older than her, had his own world of school and college friends, but in later years they were to grow close to one another and their relationship is very precious to her. Bruce was someone to be admired and

14

emulated; he was academically brilliant and a superb athlete, who was to run for his country in the Commonwealth Games. He gave her an example of high achievement that may well have influenced her future career.

To Lynn and to all her friends the great joy of Vancouver was the sea. In summer they would be there all day. They swam, sun-bathed, dug for clams in the sand, learned to prise oysters from the rocks and to clean and cook them. She loved walking with her father along the banks of the great river, the Frazer, which flows from the mountains and empties itself in the sea at Vancouver. After dinner the family often played cards: the loser would do the washing up. Lynn did not care for this; she did not, even then, like to be a loser.

At school Lynn was different from the high-spirited mischievous girl that her family and friends knew. Studying was a serious matter for her from the time she went to high school; it was important because it gave a strong foundation for her future career. Her father demanded high academic attainment: later, his greatest threat was to be that he would not allow Lynn to continue her dancing unless she made sure of top marks at school. Naturally intelligent and with great powers of concentration, she would often be found doing her homework while her friends were playing around her.

At first it is surprising to read in one of her reports that she did not mix very well with her classmates, strange indeed for someone so gregarious; then one realises that most of the children played around, but Lynn was in deadly earnest. This marks the extent of her ambition, the passionate desire to succeed that lay beneath her carefree exterior, the obdurate self-will that was to be an abiding characteristic. Later in her life one finds her accused of being dull, humourless and bent on self-improvement in a rather stiff, Victorian manner; and the contrast between this and her own vivacity, sense of fun and love of life, can only be understood if one realises that very early on she was able to negate her natural personality, even at the risk of being disliked, if by doing so she could further her ambitions. One of her teachers was a little impatient with her: in her report she was rather dismissively classified as 'ethereal and arty'. Nothing, one feels, could be less accurate—either then or now.

Even in early childhood there was, however, something mysterious and secretive about Lynn. Although she had many friends with whom she laughed and chattered—high-spirited and sometimes a bit reckless, there were reserves within her that she did not share. Her close friend, Fay Angus, remembers that 'one had to interpret silences or a flash behind her dark eyes to catch her inner feelings'. Many years later she was to be painted by Martin Battersby as a sphinx. She carries with her this sense of mystery still: there are deep silences, and one can only reach her round the edges of them; the inner world of the artist is guarded and impenetrable.

She was popular and much loved by adults for her genuine kindness and merry, carefree ways, but fortunately she was no angel. If angered beyond a certain point she hit back. An example is recalled by one of her earliest teachers. A small boy in class annoyed her greatly. Pressed beyond endurance, she retaliated with characteristic directness. She bit him. She felt no regrets because he was a horrible child and deserved it. Unfortunately it loosened her teeth for three days, but the boy was off school for a week and, to her satisfaction, returned with his arm in a sling.

Nor was she in any way inhibited. One of her delights was to support the baseball team, and going there one afternoon with her mother she was beside herself with irritation on account of the pitcher who was having a bad day. Her face red with anger, she leaped to her feet: 'Go and see your optometrist,' she yelled. She was nine years old. In later years an off-form conductor might hear something rather similar.

As a background to this fun, to the games, the hard work at school, the long summer days on the beach, there was one thing that mattered deeply to her. It was to become the centre of her life, the aim of all her endeavours. It was real and it gave meaning to all else.

At the age of six, when the family was living in Victoria, Lynn went to her first dancing class. She found life in Victoria rather boring, and her mother thought it would be a nice distraction for her. The school taught stage dancing, mainly tap, and Lynn revelled in it. Her teacher, Florence Clough, was amazed at her aptitude and at the speed with which she learned new steps. The end of term brought her first stage appearance in a large theatre in Victoria. Her mother made her costume, Lynn being somewhat demanding in matters of design. She took the stage with considerable aplomb, even stepping out of the

16

chorus line at one point to aid a colleague in some difficulty as to where exactly she should be.

When the family moved back to Vancouver, Lynn asked if she could join the evening classes given by Grace Goddard. Miss Goddard was already in her seventies; to Lynn she appeared ancient beyond belief. She taught both dancing and swimming, and usually wore a plastic bathing cap as a symbol of her dual responsibilities. It was here that Lynn heard classical music for the first time. She made such excellent progress and seemed to enjoy these classes so much that her parents enrolled her at the Rosemary Deveson Dance Studios, considered to be the best in Vancouver. Lynn needed no persuading, unlike her fellow Canadian, Jennifer Penney, now an exquisite ballerina with the Royal Ballet, who hid in the orchard rather than go to dancing school.

Carol Chambers, her close friend at that time, recalls their first class taken by Jean Jepson, a former dancer with Colonel de Basil's Ballet Russe. The children were lined up and told to point their feet. At once the beautiful arch of Lynn's foot was noticed—so much, in fact, that the teacher ran from the room to bring in her colleagues to see it.

Jean Jepson was a superb tap-dancer and taught Lynn how to break down the music into phrases when she was learning a new routine. It may well be that her wonderful musicality, apparent so early in her career, dated from this time. In addition, Jean Jepson fired the child's imagination, making her see how the theatre was another part of life to which one must be totally committed, a belief which Lynn was to hold right from the outset of her professional career. She remembers Jean Jepson well—her red hair and the fishnet tights she always wore to show off her marvellous legs. Although she was in love with the theatre, her attitude was down to earth and strictly professional, another quality that has been an abiding characteristic of her pupil. But she was also a romantic in her view of theatrical artists, seeing them as nomads, gipsy wanderers, moving across the country like the medieval strolling players; and this combination of practical good sense and professionalism, together with high ideals of the artist's calling, was to make a deep and lasting impression.

Fay Angus recalls how one summer she and Lynn, as fellow students, had the key to the Deveson studio on the top floor of Vancouver's Georgia Hotel. They would go there very early,

*Lynn, aged six, at Kits Beach. This exact pose, denoting stubbornness and rebellion, was incorporated into Kenneth MacMillan's* Anastasia *twenty-five years later.*

*A performance in the garden at home in Vancouver. The fence provides both scenery and support.*

18

between 6 and 7 a.m., to practise. They worked in complete silence and with intense concentration. Perhaps Lynn discovered here the ability to work alone that was remarked upon when she first became a professional dancer.

But she certainly was not solemn. One of her favourite jokes was imitating male dancers, of whom Robert Helpmann was the most important. Ever since she had first seen him in *The Red Shoes*, she had been fascinated by his extraordinary stage presence and theatrical magnetism; these she parodied with immense skill and not a little impudence, since she had a sharp eye for mannerisms. An important feature of these parodies would be for both girls to pinch their nostrils, let out a deep breath in order to enter on a *grand jeté* with a huge sniff.

Another favourite act was the 'mad scene' from *Giselle*. Lynn would unpin her long hair and launch into a tremendous piece of histrionics. Fay, her only audience, would sit and watch as Lynn staggered around the studio, a tiny Bernhardt with stricken eyes.

Dance activities in Vancouver were co-ordinated by the Ballet Society that organised annual dance festivals. Awards and scholarships were given through open competition. Lynn took part in these for the first time in 1949, when she was awarded third prize in her group for a solo dance. The examiner's report mentions her good technique and excellent flowing style.

In the same year, pupils of the Rosemary Deveson School took part in the annual Sun-Ray Revues, held at the International Cinema in Vancouver and sponsored by a local newspaper. Hundreds of children appeared, each performing their own items, both in group and solo dances. Lynn took part in a piece for soloist and *corps*, entitled 'Dresden'—the children nimbly imitating pieces of Dresden china. She was not the soloist: a matter which, she felt, must soon be rectified. The following year she appeared again in the review. This time she danced a tulip.

She began to take these classes more seriously, since at first they had been little more than an amusing way to spend the evening with her friends. On some evenings she and Carol arranged gala performances in the Springbetts' garden, which could be floodlit at night. A large rose trellis served the double purpose of a *barre* for practice and warming-up and as a piece of scenery to indicate some indoor aspect of the work. The choreography was improvised, with the two children meeting for momentary duets when they discussed what they should do next, but the whole garden served as a stage, so that they could cover a lot of ground.

In the latter part of her years at the Deveson School she began to take lessons from a Russian teacher, Nicolai Svetlanoff, a remarkable man whose career was one of considerable romance. He had been born in Moscow and he studied under teachers of the Imperial Ballet, subsequently travelling to Shanghai, where he became the director of the Shanghai Ballet. One of his partners was the great teacher, Vera Volkova, a favourite pupil of Agrippina Vaganova, with whom Svetlanoff danced an adagio act in Shanghai cabarets to earn a living. In John Gruen's book, *The Private World of Ballet*, Lynn gives us a portrait of Nicolai Svetlanoff:

> He had fled Moscow. You know, one of those White Russians who walked from Moscow to Manchuria. Then he went to Shanghai. Anyway, he was a fabulous teacher.... He was a real partner-type— one of those ageless, Mongolian-looking people. He had incredible eyes. You couldn't look into them. It was too much.

Lynn still remembers him vividly—the thin, almost Chinese skin, somehow ageless and transparent, drawn across his high cheek-bones, those deep, mysterious eyes. Lynn says:

> When he danced it was all joy, and I really saw very early that this was the truth of it: if it is not something wonderful, what then is the use of doing it at all?

It was her encounter with Svetlanoff that marks the true beginning of her career as a professional dancer; he was the one that made her see 'the truth of it'.

Svetlanoff imparted to her some of the concepts of the modern classical school of Russian ballet, as formed by Agrippina Vaganova and now so incomparably exemplified in the dancers of the Kirov Ballet. He showed her the openness, the flow of movement and sense of *plastique* that are the central features of the Russian school, and there is no doubt that this helped to form the extreme individuality of her

20

style. He admired her, even at so young an age, for her imagination and the creative intelligence she brought to the dance. From him she learned to take nothing on trust; every movement must be tested and explored for its meaning, as if it had never been danced before. When asked by the local press for his views on his pupil's dancing, he would reply succinctly and with great satisfaction: 'She's not a robot.'

By now Lynn was stage-struck: she adored the theatre, every aspect of it. A deep impression was made on her when she was taken to see the Ballet Russe de Monte Carlo when they danced *Coppélia* in Vancouver. The wit and elegance of Alexandra Danilova as Swanilda and the dazzling performance of Frederic Franklin, her partner, were one of the determining factors in her decision to make the ballet her career.

One evening she and Fay were enthralled to see the great Danilova sitting alone after a performance in their favourite restaurant, Scott's Café on Granville Street, where they always went for fudge sundaes. Danilova's loneliness and the sense of solitude around her moved them both. It was something Lynn was to come to know so well in later years.

They were to meet Danilova again, going backstage after a performance of *The Nutcracker*. She singled out Lynn, cupped her face in her hands and said with her marvellous Russian accent: 'Now I sign your autograph. One day I will come and see you dance Sugar Plum Fairy and then you will sign autograph for me.'

Her ambition had further crystallized by seeing the film, *The Red Shoes*. This enthralled her—the wistful, drifting beauty of Moira Shearer in the main role, the dark magnetism of Léonide Massine and the dazzling theatricality of Robert Helpmann. She could not know then how important a part in her life this great dancer and actor was to play, nor how much she would owe to him, both as an artist and a person. All she realised was that it was magic. She saw it four or five times.

In 1951 she won first prize in the solo dance competition, organised by the Ballet Society. She was to win this prize again in both 1952 and 1953, earning herself the first press notice as being a dancer 'of great promise'. In 1953 a company was formed (the first united ballet company in British Columbia, as the papers announced with some pride) to take part in the Canadian Ballet Festival in Ottawa, held in April at the Little Theatre. Its most successful work was *The Atom*,

*A student performance in Vancouver in 1954.*

choreographed for the Company by Mara McBirney. The theme was a battle between war and the atom, with the atom's commendable final decision to use his energy in the healing of sickness. As one Canadian critic wrote, 'All the dancers perform as if they themselves had tapped some new source of power.' Other roles danced by Lynn at the Festival included *Daphnis and Chloë* in which she played the role of a faun, wearing a costume mottled in brown and white, with a cap and most elegant ears.

She also danced the Winter Variation in *Cinderella*, as well as another ballet by Mara McBirney to the famous variations by Brahms on a theme of Handel. In a long report on the Festival, the critic Miss P. W. Manchester wrote of 'Lynn Springbett standing out for a miniature ballerina—with an attack astonishing in a fourteen year old, now that the days of infant phenomena are mercifully over'. Miss Manchester also described her dancing as 'one of the joys of the Festival'. Even more gratifying, she received a letter from one of the leading

American writers on the dance, editor of *Dance News* Anatole Chujoy, whom Lynn had met briefly at the Festival. In this letter he offered his help and advice to her, should she decide to make a professional career in ballet and continue her studies in New York.

Her first sight of the Sadler's Wells Ballet when they visited Vancouver made her realise that here, and nowhere else, was her real artistic home. This was the greatest ballet company she had ever seen; it was with them, none other, she would make her future. She told her mother so; in her calm and practical manner Mrs Springbett accepted the idea and did not try to discourage her. She believed that children had their own lives to live; it was not her place, either to force them or to put obstacles in their path.

Prior to the visit of the Company to Vancouver in 1953, Mara McBirney, who had been greatly impressed by Lynn's talent, had written about her to Dame Ninette de Valois in London. Sir Frederick Ashton and Ailne Phillips, one of the senior teachers at the Sadler's Wells School and personal assistant to Dame Ninette, watched her at an audition.

As the dancers came into the large, draughty hall they were all given numbers. Lynn and Fay stayed together. It was so cold they shared the same sweater, Fay's arm through one sleeve, Lynn's through the other. Sir Frederick Ashton stared at them, amazed. Throughout the whole audition he kept looking across at Lynn, as if something more than the shared sweater puzzled him.

Before this, Ailne Phillips had seen her separately. This audition took barely two minutes; neither she nor Ashton was in any doubt at all. They offered her a scholarship with the Sadler's Wells School in London. She was the only student to be accepted by the Company during their North American tour. On the day she heard the news she was invited to lunch with Margot Fonteyn. It should have been all too much for a girl of fourteen, but she acted with characteristic aplomb, posing for the photographers with her beloved dog, Amigo.

She was due to travel to England a year later in September 1954 to join the Sadler's Wells School for the winter term. Before then she took part in a talent competition organised by the Kiwanis Club of Vancouver, winning first prize in the ballet section. In June of this adventurous year she won the senior award in both the solo and *pas de quatre* competitions of the annual Dance Festival of the Ballet Society. The final excitement was her appearance in *Daphnis and Chloë* on Canadian television from Montreal with dancers from Vancouver. The great adventure of her career in Canada was over: the real test was to begin.

As a river widens, so much more mysterious becomes its source. One can see how certain events, such as her excitement over *The Red Shoes*, must have given Lynn the desire to become a professional dancer. But there is more than this. Many talented children long for a career in the ballet; few have either the resources within or the fierce determination to follow such a harsh and, in many ways, cruel road, pitted with disappointments, jealousies and blighted dreams. In what way was Lynn different from the others, what was the source of her dream?

The initial spark that was to light her ambition came early, even though one must guess at its exact nature. If her mother gave her security, warmth and love, it was her father who fostered her dreams. He had always adored his own father, the blacksmith and pioneer of Red Deer, but he had had a bad relationship with his mother. This, Lynn feels, may have led him unconsciously to resent bringing up a daughter with the normal ambitions towards domesticity, a family and children; instead, as if she were a boy, he offered another prospect—one of daring and romance. On their walks by the river together he would tell her stories about his own childhood: how he had run away from home, longing to join a travelling circus; how as a young man he used to take a job in the winter in the far north, unloading the banana trains. He described how the tarantulas, awakened by the warmth of the store sheds, would creep towards him in the half-light. He told her of his trapping line, how he would go out on icy mornings and trace the footprints of animals in the snow. Then she would listen to stories of her grandfather—of the Indians coming down before the spring thaw with furs to be traded, the river still frozen, the unshod horses slipping on the ice. He would watch for them, fifty or sixty in a group, coming over the hills.

This enthralled her. It led her to see another horizon beyond the settled, provincial calm of her city, a horizon that was full of danger, of daring and high endeavour. She could not do what her father and grandfather had done but there must be

*With Ailne Phillips of the Sadler's Wells Ballet at her audition for a scholarship, Vancouver 1953.*

another way; and in the theatre, for which she had developed an early love, she found her own world of romance. Outside the theatre, away from this intensity of life, she felt she wasted her time: the real drama was elsewhere. There were footprints in the snow.

Looking back on her childhood many years later Lynn says, 'When we're children we think a lot of things we forget about later. But they're much clearer, finer, than the things we think as adults.' In this clear, idealistic way she saw her future, shining as crystal; it was the vision of herself as an artist, though she was not to know it then, for only the artist, however muddled or murky his own life may be, retains something of a child's vision when he or she confronts the world. It is the landscape of this childhood that is never lost either to the poet or to his close spiritual companion, the dancer. As T. S. Eliot puts it:

> ... *the moment in the rose-garden,*
> *The moment in the arbour where the rain beat,*
> *The moment in the draughty church at smokefall*
> *Be remembered.*

So it was with Lynn—dancing in the garden on summer evenings, alone by the river or on the edge of the sea. The moving waters were to flow again in her dancing, the great landscape and the wide horizons of her native country were to be recalled in the grandeur of her art.

# 2: Student in London

ODAY'S THE big day!' Lynn Springbett wrote in her diary for 1st September 1954. She was due to fly to London on a morning flight. Her father had given her a sedative so that she would be able to sleep the night before. It was the day she had longed for; the day she had also dreaded.

Homesickness, like its icy companion, loneliness, is felt in advance, often long before the hour of parting, in one's most companionable and loving hours. During the previous weeks of farewell parties, presentations and excitement, surrounded by her friends, this fierce young spirit, so determined to achieve the great future she felt sure awaited her, would suddenly falter. There is a sad entry in her diary, written two weeks earlier: 'When I got to bed I felt so homesick just thinking about going that I had to get mom to sleep with me.'

The flight was delayed until evening, so she went for a walk with Bruce and her mother in Stanley Park, where she had played during so many summers of her childhood; it was, she writes, 'to take one last long look at it'.

For the great day she was dressed in style—at least in a certain style. She wore a new suit, the skirt pencil-slim, red shoes with very high heels and to complete the ensemble, a grey hat with a grey veil. She was advised by one of the stewardesses on the flight that the hat really would not do— much to her dismay—and this was left behind when she changed planes. She must, Lynn now reflects, have looked about forty-five rather than fifteen.

She had with her a letter from her maternal grandfather in which he warned her of the moral dangers that could beset a dancing girl in London, particularly from young men who would arrive at the stage door with floral tributes and evil designs. She hoped so, but thought it unlikely; stage-door Johnnies with their white ties and orchids belonged to the past.

She broke the journey in Edmonton, meeting her aunt Jean and her uncle there. Then the flight continued with one return to Montreal due to engine trouble, followed by endless hours waiting at the airport. Lynn worried more about her parents being so upset to see her leave than about herself.

Practical and self-reliant as ever, she arranged with the stewardesses that the bouquet given to her on departure should be put into the refrigerator, reminding her to see that it was removed when they changed aircraft at Winnipeg. However unhappy she might be, there was always this objective streak in Lynn's character; not only could she see to practical things, like having a shower at an hotel during the long wait at Montreal and arranging for her flowers, but she was able, even when sad, to observe her sadness and comment upon it. At times over the next few days grief almost overwhelmed her; but she could note it as something that came like a sickness, the course of which she could chart with remarkable detachment.

During the flight she wrote a letter to her mother, taking the story by stages, each composed at a different time. At Montreal she was met by two reporters and gave them her mother's address, adding in her letter that her mother must be sure to send her on a cutting of the interview. Observant as ever, she was much taken by the fact that the waiters at Shannon wore long tail coats.

Reporters were at London Airport to meet her and she dealt with them in her usual calm way. After the Trans-Canada Airlines representative had greeted her, she was taken on the coach to Victoria air terminal where one of the young teachers at the Sadler's Wells School, Gillian McIntyre, was waiting. It was all very efficiently, but rather impersonally arranged by the school. Her first remark to Gillian McIntyre was one of enormous bravado, considering how afraid she was: 'Tonight I'm going to see the ballet at Covent Garden,' she announced without so much as a quaver.

Lynn was to stay with a family at Orsett Terrace, near

---

*Lynn arrives at London Airport to begin her new career as a student with the Sadler's Wells Ballet, 1954.*

Paddington. It is a quiet, residential area with a few trees at the end of the road where it crosses Gloucester Terrace. The terrace is composed of four-storey houses with iron balconies on the first floor and more elaborate railings above the basement. The portico is pillared, quite elegantly, although the houses had certainly seen better days. A row of old-fashioned chimney pots decorated the skyline. She had a room on the fourth floor, rather larger than the one at home, and she was pleased with it, giving a detailed drawing of it in one of her letters. Several girls from the school stayed there but when she arrived she was alone with the family, thus increasing her sense of isolation.

Mr and Mrs Fisher who owned the house looked after Lynn with genuine concern. Mrs Fisher showed many kindnesses such as baking a special little muffin, the sort she loved in Canada and which she had described, and providing other little delicacies to surprise her. Lynn was able to send a reassuring telegram to her parents a few days after her arrival, describing the school as 'a dancer's paradise'. This paradise was, however, shadowed by homesickness, the dark angel at the gate.

Arnold Haskell, then Principal of the school, handled her difficulties with great tact and skill. She developed a great affection for him, a man who had devoted his whole life as a propagandist for ballet and was ideally suited to his present appointment because of his fondness for children and sympathy with their problems. She told her mother that he was the most intelligent man she had ever met—'he knows absolutely everything'—also noting that he must fix his own bow-ties as they were always crooked. He in turn showed her great kindness. She spent the evening of her first Christmas away from home at his house and was deeply touched by the two books he gave her, one on Sadler's Wells and the other on Covent Garden. Knowing her passion for ballet, he amused her with many stories of the back-stage happenings he had encountered during his career. She was enthralled. Haskell was later to take her for a week's holiday at his mother's home in Bath in order that she could rest and eat the right food—a matter that was a great worry to the authorities at the school.

Dancing was her one huge consolation. In her diary, in letters, she makes constant reference to the wonderful standards of teaching at the school, to the frightening

*Members of Winifred Edwards' class at the Sadler's Wells School.
Antoinette Sibley is in the back row on the right.*

technical prowess of her contemporaries. When she had a bad
cold it was a dreadful disappointment to miss a lesson; while
every subject, whether the *pirouette* class, or those in make-up
or mime were described as 'fascinating', 'amazingly
interesting' or 'absolutely wonderful'. The summit of her
happiness, as well as the source of her endless worries about
her limitations in technique, was the classes she took from
Winifred Edwards. Lynn adored her. 'With Miss Edwards I
understand things I've never understood before,' she writes. It
was the first of her many creative relationships with teachers
and choreographers that were to shape her career and it is
certain that Miss Edwards had an influence upon her that set
the pattern for her whole artistic development. She not only
provided her with the artistic stimulus she needed, but also on
a personal level did much to fill the huge emptiness in her
heart. She helped her in many practical ways as well, such as
showing her how to strengthen her shoes, using the same

31

method as she had been shown by Anna Pavlova when a girl in her company.

Winifred Edwards believes it is always difficult for girls coming from overseas, making the hard adjustment to a new world, many suffering from acute loneliness. It often affects their weight, already a problem because of the physical developments at puberty; an inferior diet combined with emotional stress leads to eating the wrong food as a form of compensation. Like Margot Fonteyn before her, Lynn's gifts were prematurely developed—partly, no doubt, because they had to be, since talent of this nature is a rare gift to any ballet company, particularly one with a short tradition behind it.

When Lynn Seymour was an established ballerina, she continued to have lessons with Winifred Edwards whenever she could. Miss Edwards recalls a Bank Holiday in 1961 when the school was closed so that arrangements of a slightly devious nature were necessary for Lynn and Christopher Gable to take a class with her in the little studio below the stage at Covent Garden. Winifred Edwards remarks dryly that 'the world will stop if she doesn't have a class on Bank Holiday'. Afterwards Lynn said to her, 'What we like about working with you, Miss Edwards, is that we know you think we're awful, but we always feel you think there's some hope for us.'

Miss Edwards had a wonderful class that first year, including Antoinette Sibley, even then showing the qualities that were to make her so brilliant a dancer. The standard was exceptionally high and as most of the girls had come from the Junior School, it is not surprising that Lynn felt herself rather isolated, even though they were very kind to her. But she had a different training, a slightly different style which she had learned from Svetlanoff, and there is no doubt she had much technical ground to cover before she reached the same standard as her class-mates. On the other hand she had grace, individuality, acute musical sensitivity. There was something rare and extraordinary about her dancing, glimpsed suddenly in single movements, in poses of careless beauty, magical in the eloquence of their line.

She felt over-awed by it all, but she put on her brave front, sometimes to the irritation of her companions who were often puzzled by this pretty, moon-faced little girl, so grave and secretive; indeed they did not quite know how to approach her. If she was terrified by much of the cool sophistication and the seemingly intellectual superiority of her companions, they saw her rather differently. Lynn says, 'I thought I was crumbling into the walls, but evidently I was rather bumptious.'

Dame Ninette always had total faith in this surprising child from so far away. As she says:

> From the beginning I always believed in her, and she was and is the sort of dancer I love. There was something quite special about her, and she was also very beautiful in her strange little way.

Even when so young she was independent in mind and a true individualist, but she was never a problem to Dame Ninette, who had not much patience with submissive and dutiful children in the school. As Peter Wright recalls, 'She used to grind them into a fine powder.' She admired Lynn's independence and her exceptional brain, since it was, she says, always possible to reason with her and find an intelligent response. She had the freedom of judgement that Dame Ninette has often noticed in students from the Commonwealth when they joined the school, and she has always admired the courage with which, particularly at this time when life in London was hard, drab and beset by shortages of every kind, they adapted themselves to a world so different from the one they had known. Neither the school nor the company were highly organized, since they had barely recovered from the war years and the big change of dancing at Covent Garden; it was therefore better, Dame Ninette felt, to keep up the pressure on young students from abroad, thus making the hard adjustment less of a problem to them. They would be too busy, too much involved in their life at the school to have much time for loneliness and homesickness.

There is no doubt that Lynn was fundamentally backward in terms of technique; what Dame Ninette describes as 'the three Rs', the basic groundwork of classical dancing, had been not so much neglected as passed over too lightly by her first teachers. This was then often the case with dancers first trained by Russian teachers; in their anxiety to press towards expressiveness, plasticity and freedom of movement, they neglected to lay sound foundations. Dame Ninette had the same problem with Margot Fonteyn; almost her first comment about her was that they might just be in time to save her feet. So it was with Lynn. She had beautiful feet, but they were very soft and pliable—similar to what Sir Frederick Ashton described as Fonteyn's 'pats of butter'—and it was necessary to hold her back, laboriously to rebuild her technique, if her feet were going to last.

Although the school day began at 9 am, Lynn was often there before eight. It may be that she looked upon the school as a kind of home where she could feel secure in a way that she could never be at 28 Orsett Terrace. She began to make friends with whom she went shopping and to concerts. Even at that age one is astonished by her remarkable assessment of the gifts and failings of her fellow pupils, the objectivity of her judgement. One of her first friends was Marcia Haydée—a seventeen-year-old Brazilian girl who was to become one of the greatest ballerinas of modern times, muse to one choreographer, John Cranko, as Lynn herself was to be the inspiration of another. Nobody it seemed rated Marcia all that highly at the school, where she was dismissed as 'that fat little Brazilian', but Lynn understood in a flash; indeed, seen in the light of their future development as the two greatest dramatic ballerinas of their time, this is an extraordinary glimpse into the future:

> Marcia Haydée who is from Brazil has taken my fancy. She is 17 and works so hard. We both have much the same physique and must try to improve the same things. We have a lot in common.

She found the senior girls a little strange:

> The girls are funny. They just get so ecstatic about everything, 'Oh, darling!' and 'jolly good!' are their favourite expressions.

It is typical of her that on her first day in London she visited Cyril Beaumont's ballet bookshop in Charing Cross Road. This tiny shop, in which it was barely possible to fit more than three people at a time, with its high shelves of books, the spiral staircase winding down to the basement and the small office at the back, where Beaumont could be found working under a green-shaded light in a chaos of paper, was the spiritual home for every visiting dancer and ballet-goer in London.

Tall and with his white hair *en brosse*, with a dry, measured way of speaking that quite hid his total obsession with the art, Cyril Beaumont would greet the famous and the unknown with equal courtesy, wrapping up their purchases with string and thick brown paper, his mind still half engaged in his memories of the Diaghilev Ballet and those vanished performances of long ago. If one could entice him to talk, the precise voice would quicken with memory, even tremble sometimes as he recalled the magic of Bakst's settings for the great Diaghilev production of *The Sleeping Princess* in 1921. Here Lynn took out a subscription for the magazine, *Dance and Dancers*, and bought a book on the Sadler's Wells Ballet by Cyril Beaumont, which he signed for her. She still has the book today.

Lynn hurried around London, seeing the sights, getting lost, making small, practical purchases at the big stores. London fascinated her. She enjoyed the brief encounters with those whom she considered real English types and her powers of observation missed few details in the odd behaviour of the local inhabitants:

> I got a bit confused where to go, so I went up to one of those British gentlemen with their handle-bar moustaches and asked him which way to Charing Cross Road. He then gave me a withering look and said, 'Madame, you are walking the wrong way.' Did I turn red!

She visited Westminster Abbey, Hampton Court and the National Gallery; while one of the highlights of those early weeks was a concert at the Festival Hall, not only because of the music—'so beautiful I just cried at it'—but also because of the splendid meal in the restaurant: 'quite the best I've had since I got here'. Her opinion of English food went up a little after that—but not much. She did not think much of English plumbing either: 'The toilets themselves are odd, you have to pull a little chain or string.'

Much of her sight-seeing and travelling around London was done alone, a small determined figure going to her bank, where she and the manager arranged a plan for her to save ten dollars a month; or to ballet shoemakers and into department stores to buy ribbons, belts and tapes. However unhappy she was, there is always this same practical concern for living; her imagination is kept under as close a check as are her emotions and in the diary there is little introspection or morbid imaginings.

Her greatest delights were her visits to Covent Garden. Seeing her homesickness and as a result of a call from the ever-watchful Mrs Fisher, the school arranged that she should be given passes to the theatre. Even when she went alone, as she did at first, much to the disquiet of the authorities of the school, she dressed up for the occasion.

> I dressed in my red skirt and blouse with velvet
> collar and cuffs. I wore a crinoline underneath. It
> was the nearest thing I could get to a suitable theatre
> going dress.

She was deeply impressed by most of the ballets she saw, idolised Fonteyn and was full of admiration for the other dancers. She had her own views though. Massine's ballet, *La Boutique Fantasque*, was dismissed as 'awful' and 'not even worth mentioning', while a visit to the Paris Opéra Ballet was enough to condemn Serge Lifar, the once great dancer now sadly overweight and an embarrassment to all, as 'simply terrible'. Perceptively she noted that *The Firebird* is more spectacle than choreography, though she considered Fonteyn to be 'quite brilliant' in the main role. It was strange, she thought, that the Company should have works like *La Boutique Fantasque* and *Mam'zelle Angot* in the repertoire at all.

Her real life was at the school. Slowly the loneliness abated. She had won a cruel struggle, but however much she loved classes and the academic work, she was filled with a sense of her own failings as a dancer. This, of course, was partly due to her own sense of insecurity, carried over into her work. In all her diary entries, her letters, these are her constant concern. 'I'm just not worth looking at,' she writes in her diary; or 'I was so terrible I nearly cried.' But her confidence in Miss Edwards never wavered. With her she obtained a glimpse of what the dance could mean; sudden discoveries filled her with excitement, even if it was soon to be lost again.

Her ambition, her longing for the stage, never—even at her blackest moments—deserted her. Yet apart from Winifred Edwards, who seems to have an astounding insight into her unspoken worries and fears, one gets the impression that some of those in authority at the school, who had frequent dealings with her, lacked delicacy of imagination in understanding the problems of a much-loved youngest child away from home for the first time. They were kind and considerate, but impersonally kind; one is conscious of a certain lack of spontaneity in their dealings with her. Her dreams, however, remained fixed on the future:

> It's funny, right now I'd be simply thrilled through and through if I could even be the last swan in Swan Lake!!

Whatever her doubts, the ballet staff had none: for them she was 'the wonder child', snared by the wily collector, Frederick Ashton—a rare species from a distant land. People were always coming into the studio in those early days to see this fascinating creature—in Miss Edwards' words, 'a little, slim, reed-like thing, so frail and under-developed, such a child'. Dame Ninette de Valois had no doubts at all, brushing aside Winifred Edwards' concern for some technical weaknesses. 'The child's obviously very talented,' she said at one point with a certain impatience, not wholly out of character. 'Anybody can teach talent. Talent will find its way, however badly it's taught. Nothing to it. Obviously.' Dame Ninette had no doubts about the wonder child.

But Lynn suffered from her lack of self-confidence: 'I was awful,' she writes in her diary. 'Hopeless. Had a little howl.' Her progress was, however, noted by the school with increasing satisfaction, although her physique worried them. She had marvellous feet and legs, but she was inclined to suffer from small injuries. In April 1955 she had to have an operation under anaesthetic on one foot. This she accepted with stoicism, although she complained to her mother how 'they stuck a great needle into my rear end'—which was not appreciated.

That first Christmas was not easy for her. All but one of the girls had gone home from Orsett Terrace. Miss Edwards took her to Covent Garden with Antoinette Sibley as a treat, and she was excited to see Alicia Markova in *Where the Rainbow Ends*. But it was a bad time. She was glad when term started again.

It was after her operation that she received a letter from her mother that worried her dreadfully. In it she was confronted with the choice between her career and returning home to Canada. The summer holidays were approaching and her parents felt now was the time she should make a definite decision. One can understand this, since they had been acutely worried by the many cries of homesickness in her letters; they realised that only if she made a firm, irrevocable choice would she be able to settle down to a career with a less troubled and divided mind. It may seem cruel, but as Winifred Edwards says, 'With young dancers, one must be cruel to be kind.' Lynn was aghast; she writes in her diary:

> Had disturbing letter from Mom. Have to make decision—home or career. Was upset. Had lovely class from Miss Edwards. Am in turmoil.

She thought it over and discussed it with Miss Edwards, and then wrote back to her mother. This is perhaps the most moving and remarkable of all the hundreds of letters she wrote while at school; it shows great wisdom, courage and maturity of judgement:

> I received your 2 page letter Tues and was very much disturbed by the decision you asked. I was hoping that everything was going to be taken for granted as when it's written down on paper it seems harder. My answer is—I want to return to London and the school. I've thought about it very carefully. I know that when I return from my trip home I shall feel homesick again and I will have quite a time talking myself out of it as I won't be able to say— well it won't be long, I've only six more months to go.... I'm sure I will get over it a little more quickly. ... Oh, mom it breaks my heart to make this decision, but I want to be a dancer and it's not possible to be one at home in Vancouver. If I said— right, I'll stay at home and be a normal 100% redblooded Canadian schoolgirl, after a month I'd be weeping and wailing and gnashing my teeth and would never ever forgive myself for giving up this opportunity. Being away from home and people you love is a sacrifice a dancer simply has to make.

The day she wrote this letter, there is this entry in her diary:

> Foot hurt today but was OK after warming up. Made a right mess of class—felt like having a good

38

howl. Had lunch. Walked to PO in Hammersmith with Christine. Got air letters. Wrote to mom. Watched pirouette class. Evening went to Sadler's Wells.

Neither in her diary nor her letters did she refer to the matter again.

In the final three months Lynn worked happily at the school, only anxious that the air bookings to Canada were made in good time. She was delighted to be chosen as a demonstrator to go on a Sadler's Wells summer course for teachers lasting two weeks. Dame Ninette asked Miss Edwards why Lynn was not performing the beaten steps and was told they were not strong enough to demonstrate. Not satisfied, Dame Ninette told Lynn to perform them. They were excellent, she said, quite excellent: she wondered what all the fuss was about. The child was very talented. It was quite obvious.

On 7th August 1955 Lynn flew by the polar route to Canada. Arnold Haskell had allowed her to extend her holiday until 1st October to give her ample time to rest. On 22nd September the Vancouver Ballet Society announced that Lynn Springbett was to be their guest speaker. For a sixteen year old who was something of a realist, gifted with an ironic sense of humour, this solemn announcement in the local press must surely have made her smile.

# 3: The Dark Winter

*L*YNN LEFT CANADA on 30th September 1955 to return to London. The holiday had been wonderful—sun, the sea and the watchful care of her mother, who made it clear that she was to be spoiled and cossetted during the whole period, a situation much to Lynn's taste. Then it was over. On the plane, although she put on a brave front, discovering with her usual inquisitiveness that one of the airline stewards was a dancer who had taken lessons from Svetlanoff, her resolution faltered: 'Mom, please send me a letter fast,' she wrote during the journey; 'I feel my courage running out.' But it did not; and it never has.

During the holidays she had trouble with her knee so she went to see Mr Higgs (the surgeon who had dealt with her foot operation the previous year) in his consulting room in Wimpole Street. She was impressed: 'He was wearing pinstriped trousers, and black jacket as I guess all respectable doctors in Wimpole Street do.'

For three months right up to Christmas she was unable to dance flat out. Her teachers limited the amount of work she was allowed to do; often she had just to watch difficult classes—a small, disconsolate figure, chin resting on her hand, alone in a corner of the room. Although she was not quite as homesick as before, her inner insecurity brought about periods of the most painful self-doubt:

> I wonder if I really have the stuff it takes to be a dancer. I want to have it so much.

She was easily discouraged, even misinterpreting the approval of her teachers in a manner that would seem comic if it did not hold within it so much anxiety:

40

When I was doing *port de bras* in the centre floor, Mr Plucis pointed me out twice and said that I had the right idea. What made me annoyed was that he sounded surprised.

Although they tried to be kind, the Fishers were at a loss how to deal with this moody little girl, so polite and helpful yet so distant; the troubled inner world of the developing artist lay hidden behind her watchful eyes, and they did not know how to reach it. Her loathing of English food, one of the most constant themes in her letters, remained as violent as ever:

I had dinner, some awful boiled greens, there was also a big bowl of raw cabbage and onion cut up together. Needless to say I left the greens and after sprinkling the cabbage with salt, pepper and vinegar, ate it. Was sick after! I think the Fishers' meals are better this year.

A long list of the improvements follows, set out with the greatest precision.

Behind the limited classes, the endless problems over the sheer mechanics of living, lay the terrible void of absence, the loneliness, the longing for one voice: 'I love getting your letters, mom, and when you don't have anything to say—just speak to me.'

When she took classes, she hated the sight in the mirror: 'I am just like a great gangly colt,' she wrote. 'Do you think I'll ever get a nice thin face? It's like a full moon, and so ugly.' Again, later, she remarks sadly, 'I'm an earth-bound worm.' She felt no spirit of the air, like her adored Beriosova in those ecstatic flights high above the music. In addition to this the retirement of Winifred Edwards from regular teaching at the Sadler's Wells School had left a terrible gap in her life, since Miss Edwards not only helped her as a dancer but loved her as a person. Lynn, so responsive to affection, was perhaps unhappier during this winter than at any time in her early life.

During this difficult period she was shown great kindness by Barbara Fewster, then a teacher and now Director of Balletic Studies at the school. Miss Fewster took over some of Winifred Edwards' classes and Lynn found that she gave her new perspectives and understanding of the classical dance that were to be of immense value to her in the future. Barbara

Fewster was very strict and was nicknamed the Sergeant Major. Some of the girls—most of them in fact—were terrified of her, but not Lynn: teachers have never frightened her, nor has she ever minded being shouted at if she deserves it and if she can learn something from it. Many years later, when an internationally famous ballerina, she was not at all wounded to be sent out of class by Valentina Pereyaslavec for wearing a grubby sweat-shirt. It was quite fair, she says; she never did it again.

She was devoted to her other principal teacher, Pamela May, touched by her beauty and serenity, but there was no real replacement for Miss Edwards. Her health was poor; she ate badly and the wrong things; she suffered from acute nervous tension; she could not sleep. In near despair she went to see Miss Edwards, and this restored her spirits a little. After her conversation with Lynn, Miss Edwards sent a reassuring letter to her mother who had been greatly disturbed by what she had gathered from Lynn's gloomy correspondence:

> It was a great pleasure to have Lynn here and I am very glad I was able to help her to get herself straightened out. She is a lovable child and I am very fond of her.... At the same time, I *think* a gentle hardening process must start. This is her 2nd year and she is entering a profession which requires great resilience and ability to hide your doubts and fears and make a brave show.
>
> She had a very good report at the end of her first year; she must not doubt her talent. She must accept the fact that she has technical leeway to make up; she must accept the fact that she must have patience to go forward *slowly* if she is to truly succeed.

She began to feel herself disliked by her colleagues and there was some justification for this, even though her nervous state made her exaggerate it. Her seriousness about work seemed out of place among her more frivolous companions who (it appeared to her) played around and had no dedication. This is a typical attitude in the Royal Ballet, almost a tradition, as Margot Fonteyn was to notice so many years before; it was not considered in good taste to get 'heavy' about your work, an elegant flippancy being considered more adult and sophisticated. Her earnestness bored her companions for whom the world did not begin or end with a good *arabesque*. Or so, at least, they implied; and this hurt her.

Sometimes in the dance everything came right and there was no greater joy than this:

> She gave us some terrific dance steps—the kind that the music and movement make you want to do them so badly. Oh golly, how I plunged into them and really felt I was dancing. The sheer effort and tautness you put into it made you want to cry from loving to do it so much.

After a depressing Christmas things began to look up in the New Year, when she was allowed to join the *pas de deux* classes. She could hardly sleep for excitement the night before they began, arriving at school an hour too early, maddened by her own impatience to begin. At the first class a Jugoslavian boy partnered her. She was pleased with him, except for one defect:

> The only thing was he had a powerful breath of highly seasoned foods and I nearly passed out every time I approached him.

An excitement for her was working with Terry Gilbert on his new ballet, *Spectroscope*, with music by Lennox Berkeley for the Sadler's Wells Choreographic Group. This was given its first performance on 22nd January 1956. The choreographer sent her flowers with a note: 'One day you'll be getting much bigger bouquets than this.'

In February she began to get her first walk-on parts at Covent Garden, where students at the school filled the roles of pages, courtiers or train-bearers, mainly in the classical ballets. She was one of the great crowd that backs the stage at the wedding scene in *The Firebird*. She was given a costume previously worn by an opera singer: 'I could have filled it three times,' she noted in a letter, observing that it was so loose it nearly fell off her shoulders at one performance.

In March her birthday came and she noted with some astonishment: 'I can't believe I'll be seventeen: I never thought I'd get that old.'

She continued to go to as many ballet performances as possible and was lost in wonder at Fonteyn and Beriosova, seizing on the quality that made Beriosova so superb a ballerina and which was to be her own singular gift to the future: 'Her technique,' she wrote 'is only a vehicle to carry her emotions.'

It was a dreadful six months: by late March 1956 she was again near breaking point. She was in poor health; her knees still troubled her, and she was suffering painfully from the effects of a late puberty, which was greatly exacerbated by her continual tension. Then she found a new family background; from that moment, at Easter, her fortunes began to improve.

Jill Harris first came in contact with Lynn through a cousin of her husband who ran the Ballet Society in Vancouver. At once she made it her responsibility to see that she had a home and a happy family circle where she could relax. Lynn and her friend, Jacqueline Darryl, often spent either a day there, or a weekend when they could manage it. Mrs Harris recalls how the children would go out on their bicycles for the day, returning ravenous for meals. She remembers Lynn sitting on the floor, continually flexing her feet as she stitched her ballet shoes or mended her tights—pale, tense and pitifully thin, distant within the secret worries she was so reluctant to talk about. Often she would go down alone to the village hall to practise, returning for lunch exhausted.

Mrs Harris was able to offer Lynn exactly the sort of stability and enduring affection she needed so badly at that time. In the beautiful country house near Reading Lynn found companionship with her three children—two boys, aged nineteen and seventeen, and her daughter, Rose, who was on holiday from boarding school—in an atmosphere of genuine happiness that she herself had known as a child in Vancouver.

Lynn spent a week there during her Easter holidays. She had a game of tennis with Rose, knitted and played cards. One of the boys took her to the cinema, the other played her his records. A marvellous afternoon was spent collecting primroses with Mrs Harris. She also went to a local wedding; she bought a hat with a big feather for the occasion. At last she was loved and wanted; more important, she felt a child again. Here she could be herself, the young girl who was still in need of love and protection. The fearful tension of having to act— not for a limited period but always—as if she were a mature, responsible adult was taken from her. Ever since she had come to London she had been forced to play a role that went against her entire nature; only when dancing could she be herself. Indeed she had to return to the dance to find herself, then not ashamed and guilty of being a child again.

This was at the heart of all her unhappiness: she had not been allowed to mature slowly out of childhood; it had been cut off abruptly, and so lived on in a far more intense way than it would have done had she been able to grow slowly into adult life. This conflict, between a childhood that still claimed her and the forced responsibilities which she was only capable of bearing with a great effort, had nearly destroyed her. It was the dance that saved her.

She was cruelly vulnerable and Jill Harris recognised this, responding with a genuine love that to Lynn was like the ending of the long, desolate winter of lovelessness. One can recognise the vulnerability of another when they fight to control or conceal it, most clearly seen when half hidden. This transparency of feeling was later to give her dancing its extraordinary pathos, for it had a defiant vulnerability in which she seemed to peep round the music, sly and delighted, like a child sneaking a gaze into a forbidden room. It was to this quality that great choreographers were to respond, drawn by this sense of fear and wonder in her secret eyes.

To mark this new spring in her life, two good pieces of news arrived. One delighted her; the other left her with mixed feelings. Her mother was to come over for about ten weeks in late summer, and they were to go on a coach tour of the continent together. In the same week she learned that she was to join the Sadler's Wells Opera Ballet in November 1956. At last she was to be a professional dancer, even earn a salary. But she was worried.

If students passed their final year successfully, there were four different prospects for them within the Sadler's Wells organisation. If they were exceptionally brilliant, like Antoinette Sibley, they went straight into the company at Covent Garden. The talented, with bright prospects for the future, joined the Touring Company. The competent found their way into the Covent Garden Opera Ballet and the hard workers were rewarded with a place in the Sadler's Wells Opera Ballet. This was the usual pattern, at least as understood by the dancers; Lynn, knowing this, had reason to be concerned. She saw it as a mark of failure, not realising that the main reason why she was not sent into the Touring

Company was that her teachers were concerned about her physique, particularly her weak feet, the cause of her various injuries, and her lack of strength for the demands of a large repertoire.

Peter Wright who was in charge of the Opera Ballet at the time pointed this out to her at once and she has always been grateful to him for this since it eased her anxieties about the future. Looking back on these years, Peter Wright says that it had always been Dame Ninette's view that the cream of talent available to her should be spread among the various companies in her organisation. Lynn was one of the bright hopes for the future and Sadler's Wells has always been very near her heart. It was the ideal starting point for a young dancer with a weak physique and technical limitations who could, Dame Ninette felt sure, grow slowly into her great inheritance.

Dame Ninette was also aware that in some ways she was very young for her age and felt that the more relaxed atmosphere of the Opera Ballet with fewer and less onerous performances would give her a chance to learn to live as a professional dancer, while allowing her enough time to continue to strengthen her technique at the school. Of her potential she had no doubts at all. When Dame Ninette told her mother some months later that they thought her quite exceptionally gifted, with rare qualities of movement and style, and that they did not think she would work in a *corps de ballet* for long, she also asked Mrs Springbett to keep this matter from Lynn. Obviously she did not want to raise false hopes, nor upset the other girls in the company not singled out in this manner.

Lynn in a letter to her mother was adamant: she worried because she would cease to receive any academic education from the school; engaged mostly in character dancing and walk-on parts, she would have no real opportunity to strengthen her technique, while only a few performances a week would not give her enough stage experience. 'I certainly would not be satisfied to do that sort of thing for more than six months,' she wrote with a certain hauteur. She was, however, reassured that Winifred Edwards thought it a good idea.

Before her mother arrived Lynn took a job for a week during the holidays as a waitress in a coffee bar, earning two shillings an hour. For five days this would amount to all of £4 10s. 'Not bad, eh?' she remarked in a letter. She worked the espresso machine with intermittent skill and waited on the tables, working from 6 pm to midnight. She obtained a nice bed-sitting room for them both in Hornton Street, Kensington—'the best part of London', she reported proudly. She was to work again on the summer school with de Valois, and was offered a walk-on part in the Bolshoi Ballet production of *Romeo and Juliet* when the Company made their first London appearance in October. By then her mother had arrived. Never had Lynn been happier. The dark winter was now no more than a painful memory; she was free to walk in the light again.

Peter Wright can recall vividly his first sight of Lynn the day she joined the Opera Ballet. She was wearing a green, rather long, felt skirt with a white, polo-necked sweater. She was very slim and looked pale and drawn. Then, he remembers, she vanished half-way through rehearsal; he was told she had fainted as she had been dieting too much. Lynn for her part has never forgotten how he made this motley little troupe of very young dancers straight from school—some of them, like her, very naïve and uncertain in the adult world for the first time—feel like a genuine ballet company and not, as they sometimes gloomily believed, a group of rejects from higher society at Covent Garden.

They danced two or three times a week, not only in the various operas, but also at charity and school performances that Peter Wright was able to arrange for them. He taught them how to be theatrical artists; made them interested in costume, make-up and the historical background of the operas in which they took part. Very gently, with tact and great imaginative sympathy, he turned them into professionals.

Among these young artists there was enormous potential and a number of them were later to make distinguished careers in ballet. Elizabeth Anderton became one of the leading ballerinas in the Royal Ballet touring company, celebrated for her remarkable performance in *Giselle*; she was later to be Ballet Mistress and Assistant Artistic Director of the Festival Ballet. Ben Stevenson is now the Director of the Houston Ballet in the United States. Christopher Gable, after a brilliant career as a leading dancer with the Royal Ballet, then made a new, successful beginning as an actor. Peter Wright himself, then Ballet Master of the Opera Ballet, is now Director of the Sadler's Wells Royal Ballet, after a number of important posts with the Royal Ballet and also abroad, as well as having achieved distinction as a choreographer. Lynn Seymour, as she was to become, had before her the most remarkable career of all, although the self-doubting, secretive and stubborn little girl of the Sadler's Wells Opera Ballet did not, in her black moments, even begin to envisage it.

Peter Wright had always admired Lynn, even from his first glimpse of her at the school. There was, he recalls, something exceptional about her pale beauty and fragility; he was fascinated by the elongated line she created in her dancing. 'In those early days,' he says, 'there seemed to be a slow dawning; in performance there was somehow a gauze down, but slowly she came through, marvellously.' It is interesting that exactly the same characteristic was noted by Lincoln Kirstein on his first sight of Margot Fonteyn in 1949 in a letter to Richard Buckle:

> She seems unawakened. She has a magical pall over
> her; she seems to breathe through a haze behind
> which there may be a brilliant presence, but it is not
> yet brilliantly announced.

She questioned everything she was taught—the meaning of a certain step or gesture, how it felt right or wrong to her; if necessary she would argue, even stubbornly object if something seemed incorrect. She almost, he says, demanded correction—and all that she was taught she considered, accepted or rejected with a curious certainty in her own judgement. 'She was pretty cool,' he says, 'a true individualist.' Lynn was, in her quiet determined way, trouble; and this is what both Dame Ninette and all her staff wanted. They liked a bit of fight, the demands of a fierce will in their young dancers. Artistically speaking, Lynn always gave them a run for their money. There were no short cuts for her and she would not accept any from her teachers; they had to meet her difficulties as she did, head on.

She was always willing, indeed eager, to let Peter Wright try out his choreographic ideas on her, even though these were for ballets which she was unlikely ever to dance. Her curiosity in the possibilities of creative movement was insatiable; he could come to her at any time and they would work out some new idea to see how it looked. Here he found something very important which was to be a source of inspiration for Kenneth MacMillan when he first worked with her. Her quality of movement, Peter Wright discovered, was such that even when she did something wrong, when she was off-balance or incorrectly placed, she always looked marvellous; she could make something wrong look right. This was to inspire MacMillan and other choreographers to find new imagery, brought about by seeing beauty in an academically incorrect movement, so that its novelty fired their imagination. It was what Max Ernst has called 'the divine accident'—source of new creation in many arts.

It was in late October 1956 that she was offered a part that seemed to be quite small but which was, in fact, to have a profound influence on her future and can be seen as the beginning of her career. A student group in Cambridge wished to use dancers from the Opera Ballet for scenes in their production of *Orpheus and Euridice*; Lynn was one of those chosen. The choreography was to be by Peter Wright, and her partner in a *pas de deux* danced to the flute solo in the opera was to be a young man also in the Opera Ballet, Christopher Gable.

Christopher Gable was extremely good looking with great charm and a casual air that concealed his huge determination. No one had very high hopes for him but he was a nice young man and an excellent partner. He was popular, an expert in understanding Company politics; like the rest, he enjoyed his beer and thought most of the girls in the Company a bit wet. He concealed the fact that he had endured much hardship and continual mockery from his companions in the East End of London where he was brought up, because he was training to be a dancer and thus automatically considered to be a 'cissy' or worse; and that he already had serious ideas concerning the nature of drama in ballet. He did not talk about this much: it would not have been good form.

It was to be the beginning of a famous partnership, probably the most valuable and creative in her whole career; one, certainly, that was to bring great fame to them both. Furthermore, it was to act as the central inspiration for Kenneth MacMillan who was to find in these two young dancers a new world of movement and emotion of which previously he had been unaware. But neither of them could know this as they worked together in this small *pas de deux*, performed for an amateur company in Cambridge.

At first he found Lynn rather prim, dull and provincial. To enliven their first tour some of the boys played a little game on her to amuse themselves. They would make a point of saying something indecent or shocking in Lynn's hearing, when they passed her on the stage or in class. It was quite a joke at the time. They were all very young, between sixteen and eighteen, well imbued with the Royal Ballet spirit in which it was considered very poor taste to do more than the minimum amount of work for which you were contracted. One's main concern, free for the first time, away from school and 'on the road', was with beer, sex and the football results. High-minded talk of art was not encouraged. Lynn was so very solemn. Apart from the daily class which they were all obliged to do, she worked alone for two hours in addition. They were horrified, as well as being amazed. Christopher Gable says:

> For anyone who isn't a dancer I don't think they can have any idea of what two hours of slog can mean. With no teacher, no music, no stimulus at all except just your will power, sweating and driving you along; in little church halls, in the wings, on rough floors, backstage, hanging on to bits of scenery, trying to build up this elusive strength that you can never find.

Her problems, both physical and technical, were immense and Christopher Gable came to understand them very well, as he came to understand and to love her:

> She was fighting with an appallingly difficult body which, to a greater or lesser extent, she has been fighting with her whole career. It is an amazingly fluid, flexible body that would express even then almost every nuance that she was thinking; and this, of course, is a glorious asset for a dancer to have. But the price you pay for this kind of fluidity is that the muscle structure is not built to take stress. Consequently the technique was weak at this stage.

50

She knew this very well so that she distanced herself from her colleagues.

After working with her at Cambridge, Gable began to realise there was something remarkable about this young, technically weak dancer. It was her sense of the structure of the music, its mood and texture; more than that, it was an instinctive gift for being able to reach the emotional heart of that music in a moment's insight. It was this sense of drama, found within the music, that they shared in common. It gave him respect for her and a deepening and growing affection. But in the Company, as they trailed round the provinces in the winter and spring of 1956 and 1957, she was an isolated figure, friendly with her colleagues but self-contained and reserved. The boys talked about her over their beer; they collected rude jokes to shock her. Lynn continued with her practice alone for at least two hours every day, quite unaware of their disapproval.

# 4: The Open Door

*N JUNE* 1957 Lynn wrote to her mother, 'I'm just stepping through the door to my life's ambition.' Over the coming years her interviews with the press were inclined to be offbeat and flippant; she would not risk a remark as solemn as that. But when you are eighteen years old, you speak the truth rather grandly; and this was the truth, for she did not pretend to her mother. Her promotion to the Touring Company of the Royal Ballet (as it was now known, having received the Royal Charter that year) was the realisation of a dream, invoked by a moon-faced child with braces on her teeth who, as she was to say later, spent much of her time gazing disconsolately into puddles.

The early part of the year had been difficult and uncertain. She had seen colleagues promoted from the Opera Ballet to Covent Garden or Sadler's Wells; sometimes she felt she had been forgotten completely as she battled on with her classes facing an unknown future. The brightest spot in the year had been a cabaret performance given by dancers from the Opera Ballet at Grosvenor House, where they shared top billing with a team of chimpanzees.

The Opera Ballet had not given her as many opportunities as she would have wished, although she had gained valuable stage experience. She had appeared in *Rigoletto* and *The Pearl Fishers* (in which she had to cover herself in brown paint which took ages to get off) and, of course, in *Hansel and Gretel*, where the main excitement was that at one point in the evening she had to dash off on one side of the stage as a witch, returning from the other as an angel. It was an instant transformation that had to be made while scurrying behind the set—quite a challenge—with the added possibility of tripping over some prop on the way. Looking back on those days, Lynn says: 'It was all rather tacky, like tinsel without shine.'

She had done a lot of work for Miss Edwards in connection with demonstrations for the new RAD syllabus and to her great joy had been able to take a number of private lessons from her. She had also helped Joan Benesh with practical work on the Benesh notation system of choreology, this being the first year it was taught. She learned the system herself and the notes she made at this time are still kept at the Benesh Institute. For the Cecchetti Society she danced the *pas de deux* from *Les Sylphides*, partnered by Peter Wright. It gave her great pride to be congratulated on her performance by Cyril Beaumont who told her that Fokine would have been delighted with it. But on the whole the first part of the year had been scrappy, purposeless and deeply discouraging.

In a letter to Lynn's parents Winifred Edwards wrote:

Lynn is going through a very shaky stage just now so pay no attention if she says she can't do anything! Like all young girls in their first professional year, she has lost some technical ground. It often happens in the readjustment of classroom technique to the requirements of the stage…She *is* weak, particularly in the thighs but girls of her construction always are. She will have to be patient and very determined and she should become a very beautiful dancer. The discipline of adapting herself to various stages and conditions will be good for her, although I would have liked her to have the inspiration of seeing Miss Fonteyn and the example of the soloists. Of course, as you say, in any aspect of theatre life, an artist must prove his worth. 'In Art there are no friends,' said Diaghilev. Bitter but true.

She was to join the rehearsals of the Company in July prior to their three-week season at Covent Garden, although she was not to become a contracted artist until the autumn. A joyous presage of what was to come was working with Frederick Ashton on a classical variation he composed for her as part of the RAD examination tests. Although it was a demanding piece, full of swift intricate movements, she worked very happily with Ashton, whose consideration and gentleness towards an inexperienced young artist made a great impression on her.

It was not possible for her to go home that summer but she was too busy and happy to be greatly concerned. Indeed, she could hardly wait for the first tour of the Company to begin. For the winter of 1958 the Company was to tour the provinces for sixteen weeks. They carried a repertoire of both classical and modern works, including *Coppélia, Les Sylphides, Pineapple Poll, Veneziana, Blood Wedding, Les Patineurs* and *Solitaire*. At the same time the Company was to learn four new ballets on tour, three entirely new works and one reconstruction of an existing ballet. This was a staggering schedule, particularly with the difficulties of finding rehearsal time and space, to say nothing of unsuitable stages on which to work. They were to dance eight performances a week, four of these being given over to the works of young choreographers. She would have about three weeks to learn practically her entire repertoire. It was a huge challenge for Lynn, just what she wanted.

John Field, the director of the Sadler's Wells Theatre Ballet (as the company was then called) had a different impression of Lynn from that formed by the boys in the Opera Ballet. Although he agrees she was unlike the other girls, in no way did he consider her dowdy or unattractive; indeed he remembers her as being 'rather exotic and certainly a very beautiful girl'. He noticed, however, the same characteristics: the acute, questioning mind, the continual self-doubt and impatience with herself, the demand for a kind of instant perfection for which she had not the patience to wait. Morale-boosting sessions from him became essential. The problem was that she wanted to be a great dancer tomorrow, so that he had to ask her to hold on at least until the weekend. In this manner, he assured her, the seemingly interminable wait for greatness could be endured, even as long as the three or four days necessary to attain it.

His empathy with young artists made him an inspiration to his dancers and he recognised her gifts at once. Her development as a dramatic ballerina rather than a pure classical dancer stemmed, he feels, both from a need to find a different way, owing to her technical limitations and her exaggeration of these in her own mind, which was the conscious decision of a very intelligent girl, and also from her own personality that could find expression only through the drama. The dance was her voice; only through it could she reach the depths of her nature.

There is in her temperament, as noticeable then as now, a curious duality between the gregarious, outspoken and often blunt human being, so warm and exuberant, and the secretive, rather isolated woman for whom this outward charm is a mask that hides the lonely, unquiet spirit within that searches, so unavailingly, for a place and a heart to rest in.

John Field was the ideal director for this company, filled with young, dedicated and searching dancers. His warmth of character and understanding of their personal and artistic problems, coupled with his enthusiasm and integrity, inspired them to develop both as artists and maturing young people in an astonishingly rapid time, without forcing them to excess nor holding back their eagerness to experiment. He won their loyalty, retained their respect and affection and built the Sadler's Wells Theatre Ballet into a company of marked individuality. Nothing enraged the dancers more than to describe them as 'the second company'; even today, so many years later, former members of the Theatre Ballet can still be made to bristle at such a comparison. In their eyes they were second to none. John Field encouraged them to believe this, to dance in that belief; and they responded to him with total conviction in their own worth. The Royal Ballet owes a great debt to him as it does to that eager group of dancers who found their identity and sense of purpose far away from the Opera House at Covent Garden.

The first role Lynn learned was in *Les Sylphides*, and by the end of the tour she had danced almost every *corps de ballet* part in the repertoire. She understudied in *Solitaire*, which in later years was to be so closely associated with her, while Peter Wright gave her a role as one of the six couples in his new ballet, *A Blue Rose*. This was a slight work, loosely constructed on the idea of a rose being passed from one dancer to another. She had enormous delight in dancing the tarantella in Andrée Howard's *Veneziana*, and then appeared as one of the dotty, love-sick girls in *Pineapple Poll*, which gave audiences the first glimpse of her zany sense of humour. She worked hard, enjoyed the challenge of so much to be learned of this big repertoire, where a certain amount of improvisation and swift costume changes were necessary since the Company was so small. In the third act of *Coppélia*, for example, the *corps de ballet* had to dance both the Morning and Evening Hours in the *divertissement*, changing their costumes in the wings. It was a huge challenge for Lynn and she adored it. Sometimes she fell foul of the Ballet Master, Henry Legerton, a strict disciplinarian and a dear friend of hers; once, she recalls, he really yelled at her for chewing gum while being a Tree in *Blood Wedding*.

The Company were to open their own season at Covent Garden on Boxing Day when she appeared in both *A Blue Rose* and *The Angels*, an inferior piece by John Cranko, but at least she had the privilege of making her first London appearance with the Company at two premières. But the main event of the season was to follow.

As a choreographer Kenneth MacMillan was already beginning to make a major reputation. His first ballets, *Danses Concertantes*, *House of Birds* and *Noctambules*, indicated a brilliant talent. His style was spiky, elegant and witty on the one hand, while in addition he had a dark, brooding imagination that produced works that seemed curiously objective and lacking in warmth. His style was compressed and epigrammatic; but it was tense, lacking flow and emotional colour. His critics said they were brilliant but heartless ballets. Perhaps he needed a certain type of dancer, a quality of movement and personal style to enrich his marvellous plastic imagination that seemed to be little influenced by his contemporaries or his predecessors.

MacMillan chose Lynn from the *corps de ballet* to dance the role of one of two adolescents in his new ballet, *The Burrow*, which was to be performed during this season. He has never forgotten his first, astounding encounter with Lynn which, to so large an extent, formed the pattern of their two careers. Looking back, still in some amazement, over a gap of twenty-one years, he says:

> I saw her for the first time at a rehearsal of Peter Wright's ballet *A Blue Rose*. She did one movement, and it struck me that I had never seen a dancer do a movement so beautifully before. It was a *temps levé* in arabesque which is one of the simplest steps in the

whole vocabulary of dance. Yet it had a freedom that young dancers then didn't possess; it was like that of a Russian dancer.

When other dancers read this, MacMillan says, they will probably burst out laughing, because the step is so basic, so absurdly simple. There is nothing to it; and so he would have thought himself; but when he watched Lynn perform it, there was a world there, a world he did not previously know existed. Somewhat baffled by his own reaction, he chose her for this small part in his new ballet, perhaps even then beginning to doubt what he had seen, this mirage of beauty across the dry lands of the academic technique.

When they came to work together, they discovered a mysterious rapport between them on an instinctive level which had nothing to do with the normal verbal and visual communication between a choreographer and a dancer. 'It was,' he says, 'as if we shared the same brain. She would come to the same conclusion as I would about a movement at exactly the same time. It was uncanny. I don't know how it happened, and I still don't know.'

He realised that it had something to do with her extraordinary musicality, so close to his own; they were to find the same imagery in the music as if with a shared imagination. And this rapport was not something that grew up between them as they worked together on *The Burrow*; it existed from the outset, a reality from the creation of the first steps. They found it before they had even had time to seek it. He looked at her during breaks in rehearsals rather as Frederick Ashton had done at that first audition, amazed.

They also discovered that they shared many of the same ideas about the nature of the dance: that it should be dramatic, theatrical, not merely an abstract patterning of steps, but the expression of emotion and mood to be felt by an audience. As MacMillan says:

> She is and always has been so musical. I can set a step to music and she will say, 'Why don't we do it this way on the music?' in a totally different manner. She can play around with music. She feels it so much in her body and through her body. I just have to say, 'Go in that direction' and she goes. I don't mean just physically, but mentally as well. She is so receptive,

and she has a divine body; the instrument is truly wonderful.

MacMillan saw in this solemn child a hint of something rare and mysterious; it belonged to her silky, almost voluptuous way of moving, so that the music seemed to undulate around her floating limbs. To him she seemed perfect for the images of awakening love that he planned to create. For her he began to compose slow, drifting little dances, fragmented like broken sighs, hesitant like those words a young girl in love does not trust to the air but lets trail away unsaid. It was something new in his choreography, very small in its beginning and with a tenderness he had not shown before.

The ballet was not unlike *The Diary of Anne Frank* in mood, a stage version of which had been seen in London, dealing with a group of people forced to live in hiding in one small room. It is a claustrophobic work in which one senses the repressed anger, the neurotic terror and the terrible fear that haunts each of the characters—all except the adolescents, too lost in one another to realise what is happening, for whom the first kiss is more momentous than the fearful knocking on the door that ends the ballet. So much of the character was herself: this odd mixture of shyness and maturity, of innocence and a quiet wisdom that lay beneath it; the girl who is so contained and yet so full of feeling. One cannot doubt that the choreography, particularly in the beautiful double work, grew from the personality of MacMillan's young dancer with whom he worked in such accord.

Donald MacLeary was a wonderful partner in this and many other ballets that they danced together; indeed he was one of the finest ever produced by the Royal Ballet—musical, strong and sensitive, with an instinctive understanding for the individual qualities of movement of each of the dancers he supported. Lynn picked him out at once as the ideal partner, going up to him immediately and asking him to practise some double work with her. Although this was pretty cheeky from a new member of the *corps de ballet*, MacLeary agreed to help without a hint of reproach. Often after that they practised together; from this a devoted and lasting friendship was to develop.

*The Burrow* was given its first performance, attended by Princess Margaret, on 2nd January 1958. The audience roared

*Lynn's first created role, in* The Burrow, *with Donald MacLeary, as the two adolescents in love, 1958.*

their approval through eighteen curtain calls. Lynn and her partner took a separate call in front of the curtain. It was a triumph for the Touring Company and for its new recruit, dancing a soloist role after only three months in the *corps de ballet*.

While working with MacMillan on the ballet, Lynn had been prodded both by him and by Dame Ninette into making a change which was not very popular at home. Dame Ninette had said in her brisk, no-nonsense voice, 'Springbett's no name for an Odette/Odile: you must change it.' MacMillan backed her up. Lynn wrote to her mother:

> Ken MacMillan thinks I ought to change my name. How do you think LYNN SEYMOUR sounds and looks in print? If you can think of any super suitable French Canadian name that you'd like better—send me a telegram.

This rebirth took place during the Company's Christmas party in Hull, a place for which she has no other memories except that there were horrific bed bugs at her 'digs'. This was the rough aspect of touring: bleak northern towns in a dirty drizzle of rain, a theatre with a ferocious stage rake, cold or damp hotels and boarding houses—all these things were not entirely conducive to high artistic endeavour. But she loved it: she was a true professional at last.

Her next letter to her parents had written on the back with her address, 'Lynn Seymour'. They did not like it.

After such a triumphant night and the wide publicity that followed it there was a sense of anti-climax when the Company began their next provincial tour. Prior to that, Lynn had been presented to the Queen Mother at a Gala performance and found her very charming. 'Of course I had to make a complete idiot of myself,' she adds, omitting any reason.

Winifred Edwards had written to Mrs Springbett to tell her of Lynn's first big role at Covent Garden. She had found her 'much more grown-up and thoughtful', while she thought her interpretation in *The Burrow* excellent, adding, 'the role is so much what she is'. Critical comment on the new ballet had on the whole been favourable, although Lynn, like most dancers, was far more interested in the reactions of the audience than in those of the critics. Most of the reviewers gave a favourable mention to the new dancer; one comment (from *Dance and Dancers*) is particularly interesting:

> Lynn Seymour is an especially beautiful dancer, having a warmer, more lusciously individual appeal than any young English girl I have seen in ballet since June Brae held the audience with her curiously penetrating femininity twenty years ago.

A pleasant interlude in the grinding routine of a long tour was the work she and some other dancers did in their spare time on a new ballet by Alan Beale, a dancer in the Company; this was presented by the newly-formed Sunday Ballet Club at Wyndham's Theatre on 23rd March 1958. It was a thin, plotless work, but with a stylish *pas de deux* for herself and Donald MacLeary. The ballet was coolly received, but Lynn described it all as 'good fun'. (Her friend and flat-mate, Jacqueline Darryl, a South African girl now in the *corps de ballet* of the main company, appeared during the same evening in a ballet by David Drew and with characteristic generosity, Lynn was very excited by her performance.) A critic in *Dance and Dancers* was impressed:

> ...the Canadian girl, Lynn Seymour, showed perhaps more clearly than ever that hers, properly used, could develop into a very considerable talent.

On the next tour she danced her first solo: that of Dawn in the third act of *Coppélia*, a difficult piece demanding the utmost precision in classical style and good elevation. She felt she had neither. Also she thought she was putting on weight again, a recurrent worry when she became discouraged about her performances. 'I'm dancing hideously and fat as a cow,' she told her mother. The problem of her weight has recurred throughout her career and periodically she has suffered much from having to go on spartan crash diets. It was not in this case that she had become overweight; she just felt fat, which for her is the same thing. When her colleagues remarked on how thin she looked, she was always amazed. It is possible that the weight problem, a cruel difficulty at certain times in her career, also acted as a subconscious compensation and an excuse for her limitations which she would never dream of making in a conscious manner.

A week's interlude between tours allowed her the luxury of private lessons from Winifred Edwards who was not in the least disturbed by a certain technical decline in her dancing. The effect of her teaching was, as ever, to rekindle Lynn's enthusiasm and to reinforce her courage. Lynn writes:

> She's the most vital and wonderful person I've ever met.... Now I'm thinner, encouraged, inspired and dancing better.

One of her most exacting tasks was to learn the intricate *pas de trois* in *Swan Lake*, since this requires both speed and great precision. She also danced the exquisite *pas de trois*, set to a song by Fauré, in Andrée Howard's ballet *La Fête Etrange*. She danced this when the Company visited Ireland, and she adored the life in Dublin—so relaxed, friendly and natural. Indeed she took to the Irish, since their nature was like her own, in contrast to the English who were sometimes inclined to be shocked by her Canadian openness and lack of reticence. She was not renowned for tact. Although she was still not greatly liked in the Company, her performance in *The Burrow* had impressed her colleagues; they were quite willing to recognise that she was a remarkable artist in the making and they had great respect for her professionalism. But she could relax in Dublin: 'The Irish are gentle and obliging and ever so slightly mad.'

Dame Ninette de Valois visited the Company when they were on tour and was able to announce that they were to be given a salary increase of £1 10s a week. This went down very well, although they had to admit it was not a princely sum; indeed one or two of them grumbled a bit—but well out of Dame Ninette's hearing. Like all the dancers of the Royal Ballet from its earliest days until now they both loved and were scared stiff of her in about equal measure; and no doubt she thought this a very proper attitude. Over the years legends have sprung up of her kindness, her rages, her unpredictability and her astonishing vagueness. The dancers cherish her for this, as much as for her brilliant intellect, her genuine compassion and integrity of purpose.

In July Lynn went on holiday in Vancouver. It was marvellous. She swam, she lazed in the sun, and ate innumerable ice creams. It was as difficult as ever to adjust to her loneliness when she returned, for she knew it would be a long time before she saw her mother again. The most exciting of all their tours was to begin: eight months in Australia and New Zealand. It was to mark a turning point in her life, both as an artist and a person.

# 5: To Australia

*T*HE COMPANY TRAVELLED to Australia by air, leaving London on Friday 29th August 1958 and flying via Frankfurt, Cairo, Calcutta, Bangkok and Singapore. They arrived in the evening of Tuesday 2nd September. Few more exhausted and dishevelled groups can have emerged, blinking into the light and facing a battery of cameras, than the unfortunate young dancers of the Royal Ballet. Some of them were eighteen and nineteen years old; for a few this was their first trip abroad, while even a seasoned traveller like Lynn felt tired beyond belief. Typically, her immediate reaction was an urge to get working again as soon as possible.

She had been the only member of the Company not upset or excited at the prospect of the tour; as she observed laconically: 'I wasn't leaving anyone and not going to anyone.' Nor was she particularly disturbed by the statement of John Field that anyone who missed the plane would be waiting for eight months in London without pay. It had been enough to keep some of them awake all night prior to departure.

It was a considerable risk to send a young, inexperienced company to Australia and New Zealand, since the fact that this was thought of as the *second* Royal Ballet group did not endear them to the critics or the public who at first felt slighted. The repertoire was a careful balance between the old classics and modern works. It contained *Swan Lake*, *Giselle*, *Coppélia* and *Les*

---

*As Odette in one of her early performances of* Swan Lake. *This was the first full-length classical role Lynn had ever danced, her first performance in Australia in 1958.*

*Sylphides*; the modern ballets were *The Burrow, Hamlet, Façade, A Blue Rose, Pineapple Poll, Veneziana, Blood Wedding, The Rake's Progress* and *Les Patineurs*. The leading ballerinas from Covent Garden with their partners were to join them on different stages of the tour that was to open in Sydney, and then continue to Melbourne, Adelaide and Brisbane before visiting New Zealand.

The dancers were welcomed with generous hospitality but audiences in Sydney were poor and the press hostile. Dame Ninette was with them for the first few weeks to see that they had settled in all right, for she was aware of the strain put upon her young and mainly inexperienced dancers—'the cosmopolitan teenagers', as one newspaper charmingly described them. She began to give Lynn extra classes to which she responded with delight. First she had to work on the difficult *pas de trois* in Act I of *Swan Lake*:

> It's the world's worst test piece for endurance, and yet it has to be full of charm because of its choreography.

Then Dame Ninette told her she was to learn the role of Odette/Odile in *Swan Lake*. Lynn was stunned. She telegraphed the amazing news to her parents, and then wrote to them:

> I still can't believe it. This will be the greatest moment in my life. Sometimes I get in an awful panic and wonder if I'll ever get through it. I've never even been tried for a leading role in a one-acter, let alone a four-acter.

No wonder in those early weeks, encouraged, coaxed and bullied by de Valois, she wore out two pairs of shoes a day. She was at her happiest—overworked and overstretched as an artist. She describes herself with a kind of grim delight as being 'a living wreck', adding, 'I seem to be in tears after every performance.'

Dame Ninette had no doubts; they were not something she had ever much encouraged, either in others and certainly not in herself. If other people thought that perhaps she was forcing a young, inexperienced dancer too fast, making her perform a role that taxes even the greatest ballerinas at the height of their powers, it was just unfortunate that in this case they were mistaken. She had achieved it with the gauche, technically weak Margot Fonteyn and she would do it again; talent, as she often remarked, would find its way, once she had put it on the right road. Lynn was relieved of all her small parts and most of the *corps de ballet* work so that she should concentrate on Odette/Odile; at the same time Dame Ninette insisted that in order to strengthen her technique Lynn should dance the *Don Quixote* duet, probably the most exacting piece of technical bravura in the entire classical repertoire, partnered by a somewhat reluctant Donald Britton.

Towards the end of the season in Sydney, de Valois returned to England. Lynn was distraught; learning the most difficult of all classical roles, she was left on her own:

> If only Madam could have stayed on or MacMillan had been here. We're desolate of her inspiring personality.

She was unhappy, with few roles and no one to give her much help in all the details involved in the huge part of Odette/Odile, although here Rowena Jackson, one of the ballerinas of the Company, gave her additional private coaching. This was exactly the sort of practical advice she needed, dealing with matters of timing, use of the stage and the spacing of energy. As far as the character and the inter-relationship between Odette and Odile were concerned she was content to let them work out their own meaning on the stage; it would be sufficient just to be able to cope with the technical demands of the role.

Her colleagues grew at times a little impatient of her anxieties. She recalls how she was somewhat taken aback when she complained to one of the older members of the company that she should never have been asked to do the role and that she would be hopeless in it, to be met by the calm response: 'Yes, I entirely agree. But you've got to do it.' After such a remark terror settled like ice round her heart.

John Field took many of her rehearsals for the role, but it was a hard time for her as these had to take place before general class in the morning which meant a very early start to a long day. He continued to reassure her. 'I always trusted him,' she says.

Of course she was getting fat again. She knew the reason:

It's all mental. When I'm happy I'm slim, fat when I'm sad ... the more I put on, the more I indulge ... I need someone. I've done so little, it's a crime.

Her first two performances in *Swan Lake* were to be the matinées on 12th and 15th November in Melbourne. She could not quite believe it as the time grew closer and no one seemed particularly concerned.

One of her greatest disappointments was that at the last minute it had been decided that Kenneth MacMillan was not to travel with the Company and mount two new ballets as previously arranged. Through working together on *The Burrow* they had become friends; indeed she thought she might even be in love with him, so acute was her response to his gentleness and consideration, but on reflection she considered that this was as likely to be a 'crush' as a romance. Lynn wrote about him to Carol Chambers before she left for Australia.

Ken MacMillan is showing promise! To begin with he will be coming with us for Australia. It still may be a crush but I feel like a goner.... He's a person fantastically aware of other people's emotions— almost psychic, amazingly kind and gentle.

Their relationship was something she has always needed, a man from whom she could learn, on whose talent she could feed and be enriched both as an artist and a human being; above all, one who had the imaginative sympathy to see the flowering of amazing gifts within this rather enclosed, shy young girl, who was not much liked or understood by her colleagues. MacMillan had glimpsed her potential and it quickened his imagination, broadened the range of his art. She refers to this very beautifully in a letter to Carol:

I am merely a young person to whom God or whoever it is had let him perceive a quality or something in my work which hits a chord and agrees with him.... I discovered my joy in being with him was really due to his way of transmitting *his* world to me and greatly appreciating what *I* had to offer him. You can imagine how my heart soared with that realisation.

Always she has loved the company of those of great talent—writers, painters and musicians—and has never ceased to learn from them. Kenneth MacMillan was one of the first of these; and it is for his gifts, as much as for his qualities as a human being, that she loved him: 'Dear Ken—divine character, fabulous personality.'

The Australian tour was also to see the beginning of another friendship that was to have a profound influence both on her art and on her personal style of life. Robert Helpmann had joined the Company in Melbourne during November as a guest artist. At that time he was also playing in Noël Coward's *Nude with Violin* in Australia and New Zealand, and managed to fit in performances with the Royal Ballet during breaks in the tour of the play. It was natural that Lynn should respond to a man so gifted—actor, dancer, choreographer—who was also witty, intelligent and worldly-wise. Lynn was fascinated by him: 'It's all I can do to keep myself from following him about like a puppy dog.'

Sir Robert Helpmann remembers vividly his first impression of Lynn at that time:

> I was present at a rehearsal of Kenneth MacMillan's ballet *The Burrow*, when on the stage appeared one of the most exciting scenes I have ever seen, a young, powerful, dramatic actress, as well as a beautiful dancer. I was thrilled at the sight of her and I asked her name and was told it was Lynn Seymour.
>
> My interest in ballet has always been on the side of the drama and therefore to see somebody fufil everything that I believed ballet should have was to me one of the most exciting experiences.
>
> During the tour I became, and still am, a devoted friend. Lynn's sense of humour, her sense of theatre, her sense of friendship, is something that I will value deeply all my life.

As Helpmann's biographer, Elizabeth Salter, reports, the invitation to appear with the Company had been put to him by Dame Ninette de Valois in her usual forceful way. She wrote to Helpmann:

> Since you're going to be over there anyway it seems

stupid not to dance with us again. It will be so easy
and convenient.

The choice of adjectives must have caused Helpmann to
smile, since to be obliged to cover great distances between play
and ballet, fitting in two different schedules, was not perhaps
quite so easy and convenient as all that. But of course it could
be achieved—just, that is by a man with his huge stamina; he
had done it before when he spent a season alternating
between plays at Stratford and ballets at Covent Garden. He
would not go into such irrelevancies with Dame Ninette,
naturally.

It is typical of him that he sought never to intrude upon
John Field's responsibilities as director of the Company,
always seeking his permission before giving private coaching
to the dancers, always concerned lest it should be thought he
was exceeding his authority, since as far as Helpmann was
concerned he considered himself one of the dancers and no
more than that. The fact that John Field was a very junior
member of the Sadler's Wells Ballet when he was its leading
dancer never crossed Helpmann's mind.

The two of them, Lynn and Sir Robert, became close
friends; they were always together—the great man of the
theatre, forty-nine years old, and the young dancer, so
inexperienced in life and so inexpert at living it, who was not
yet twenty. He recognised her gifts immediately, just as he was
touched by her eagerness to learn from him. Lynn had
discovered a rare, unexpected friend:

I have felt the need to always be with him—hearing
him speak and have ideas flowing over me in
refreshing wave after wave.

At Melbourne things brightened up a good deal. Audiences
were better, the critics kinder. Also she had found new friends.
Mr and Mrs Casson welcomed her to their home, where she
could sleep, listen to music, eat home-cooked food, and hear
stories of Sir Lewis Casson, Dame Sybil Thorndike and the
great world beyond the ballet. But she was gloomy, even a bit
cynical: 'Tour prospects next year are either North America
or Russia, but will probably be the provinces.'

Two of the principal dancers, both Australian girls, Brenda
Boulton and Margaret Lee, took her under their wings; they

not only helped her with her work—the approaching *Swan Lake* still filled her with terror—but they also made her feel more at home in this strange land whose great spaces, the beaches and the sea reminded her so poignantly of her own country. At this stage in her life she felt lost, unsure of her nature. As she recalls:

> I had no real perspective on life. There was only my work. Then it was the whole of my life, and when that wasn't going well, it was terrible because I had nothing. I felt in a way homeless.

She was scared stiff by Odette/Odile. 'Shall I jump on a train to nowhere?' she wrote. Miss Edwards would disapprove, she knew, believing she was too young and too weak technically for the role: 'I haven't dared to tell her yet. She'd hit the roof about it.' But her fierce capacity for work never relaxed. Even on the occasional free day she would insist on lessons either from John Field or a member of the Company staff; in the end they had to lie to her, saying that even if she wanted to work they needed their day off and she would just have to rest like all the others. She would accept this, although reluctantly.

There were, however, diversions. She watched as affairs began to proliferate within the Company; rumours seethed as romances formed and crumpled even before the gossip had time to settle. It amused her. She wrote to a friend with all the cool, detached wisdom of nineteen years:

> Lots of affairs have started up out of the blue. All the new kids are really letting rip (17-18-19 year olds), it's fantastic. They must have had terribly oppressed childhoods or something. Also two of the eldest old maids and frustrated type girls are now entangled! Great dramas all over the place.... So our little group has suddenly blossomed forth from the moral touring company to a seething mass of love. For God's sake don't breath a word to mom and dad, they'd have a fit!!

Anya Linden, one of the principals from Covent Garden, had now joined them and she and Lynn became great friends. Not only an exquisite dancer, Anya Linden was also a bit of a nonconformist. She was considered very modern and daring in her ways; rumour had it that she sunbathed in the nude.

Then it was 12th November 1958. On the day of the matinée the Canadian flag was hoisted above the theatre. This was on the instructions of the late John Scarlett, the public relations officer, a devoted admirer of Lynn. Judging by her terror and morbid imaginings before the performance, she probably thought it should have been flown at half-mast.

The performance was, in fact, a magnificent début. Although it did not conceal all her technical weaknesses—particularly in the pyrotechnics of Act III—she danced with such purity of style, so majestic a flow of movement in the shaping of the musical phrases that both critics and public were entranced. The notorious *fouettés* defeated her and she only managed to complete eight of the thirty-two. At her next performance she doubled the number; in each case her experienced partner, David Blair, filled in her music with majestic aplomb. The third performance, however, was to mark the début of Donald MacLeary in the role; and he was just as nervous as his ballerina. At rehearsal, when she had reached the twelfth *fouetté*, MacLeary leaped forwards to fill in the expected gap. However the nervous tension was too much for him and he fainted in a heap on the stage. That did the trick. At the performance Lynn completed, for the first time ever, all thirty-two *fouettés*, steeled in her endeavour by the thought that otherwise he might pass out again. 'It was more or less moral blackmail,' she says.

She tells the story best to her mother, having previously sent her a laconic cable that just said: PERFORMANCE SUCCESSFUL. RELIEF.

In the letter she was more expansive:

> The biggest thing *ever* is now over for awhile. First performance of *Lac* was such an experience—the times I nearly crumpled and lost heart. I did some very bad things but when I mentioned them, half had been forgotten. The audience was full of supporters and the Company with me all the way. At the end the relief was terrific and the kids gave me a hand! ... I did a dreadful 2nd Act variation but 3rd Act was better....

The most imaginative tribute she received was a large cake with one candle on it from Lady Tate of the Tate and Lyle company. This touched her, particularly the symbolism of the one candle. It gave her great joy that the Company rallied round to help her through the performance. She was partnered immaculately by David Blair, whose experience and understanding of the role were of immense value to her. Indeed the Company was proud of their new Odette and impressed by the shy and modest way in which she accepted her success.

At last she plucked up courage to write to Miss Edwards, having learned to her horror from Dame Ninette that she had already told her about it:

> Madam reported that you looked faint! You can imagine the turn my heart gave when the news was received shortly after our opening in Sydney.... At times, most times, courage was simply drained from me. Imagine doing the whole of *Lac* when you're still incapable of standing on one leg! I had about eight weeks to work on it.... Honestly, I did do everything in my power as far as thought and labour was concerned. But then as now I was simply crying out for guidance. Svetlana was sweet but frightening. I had a dress rehearsal on the day before the performance and that was the all-time low. The performance finally arrived and was over. I did some dreadful things, David Blair carried me through. It was a wonderful occasion in my life. I hope I don't disappoint anybody. Sometimes it just seems too much....

To those who protested that Lynn had not the physique or technical resources for a classical ballerina, Dame Ninette was calmly dismissive. She was not nor ever will be a virtuoso dancer but her technique was fully adequate for all the classics. 'She was and is purity itself when it comes to classicism,' Ninette de Valois says. Maybe, Dame Ninette says, 'she did a lot of things a bit too soon,' but great talent can be hindered, even destroyed, if held back too much in a nature desperately eager to give it expression. Lynn has always been profoundly grateful that she was allowed to dance all the big classical roles so early in her career, thus being spared the discouragement, the loss of inspiration that have been the misfortune of dancers who did not reach the great roles until much later.

There seems, however, to be common agreement—notably between Dame Ninette herself, Winifred Edwards and Kenneth MacMillan—that Lynn was pushed ahead rather too fast, and this is particularly true in the classical ballets. As MacMillan says:

> The way she dances is not the way people here in England want to see the classics. They are, or perhaps were, a bit prejudiced about the way they think they should be done. She was not happy in them as she was unable to find realistic truth in them, for they have no realistic truth; the accent is wholly on the dancing. Yet she was always looking for it and never finding it. Further, the critics really have misunderstood a lot of her work. Because she is such a great dramatic artist, she convinces them so much that they forget about the dancing when she is actually a wonderful dancer.

As we shall see later, it was not until Lynn started working with Rudolf Nureyev on the classical ballets that she began to find the truth of them. It is, perhaps, that brought up in the same Russian school he provided for her the link between herself and Svetlanoff which had been weakened over the many years of dancing within a different background. It was only then that she realised she had been looking at the classics in the wrong way; when she learned to understand them differently she was, at last, and perhaps for the first time, at ease and happy within them. It is certain, Kenneth MacMillan believes, that her early problems with the classics, brought about by dancing them with insufficient technical preparation, may permanently have damaged her confidence as a classical ballerina. Her inner doubts were reinforced, so that she was something like a patient who believes he is seriously ill, while every attempt to reassure him is taken as a means of trying to conceal that truth from him, rather than as an objective statement of fact. She believed what Kenneth MacMillan told her but this lack of self-confidence made her doubt everyone else, even those like Dame Ninette, Winifred Edwards and John Field, whom she so greatly trusted.

Lynn was much happier in Melbourne than in Sydney, being very fond of the city and its setting. Shortly after the performance the whole Company went to a civic reception; it was all very grand, Lynn reported, adding with some satisfaction that she up-staged the other girls 'in their sophisticated numbers' by wearing her new poppy dress. Another treat was a party given by French naval officers on board their frigate, prior to their departure for Tahiti the next day. They were, not unexpectedly, charming; some of the girls, already love-smitten, were troubled anew. It was a marvellous party, breaking up near dawn, a few hours before class and two performances the next day. Lynn was delighted to be told by one of the French officers that they did nothing and got up very early to do it. 'Very French,' she noted with approval.

Lynn danced Odette/Odile at eight more performances in Australia and New Zealand, partnered by Donald MacLeary. At each, her interpretation of the dual role began to gain in poignancy and depth. Critical reception was excellent; one writer said very nicely that 'she invested it with the beauty of driven snow'. In an interview with the press, Robert Helpmann spoke with great enthusiasm about her: 'She is a wonderful person. A truly great talent, and one of the few ballerinas.'

She was by now herself quite an old hand at giving interviews, but no one could be less of the big star, even when she received top billing with the ballerinas for the New Zealand part of the tour; and few things were to irritate her more than the justifiable but somewhat extravagant shouts of triumph that began to clamour in the Vancouver press: 'It all sounds a bit phoney to me.' The more sophisticated *Dancing Times* of London was more accurate in describing her as 'not yet, of course, a swan queen; she is more like an enchanting baby princess'.

Lynn was quite sure what she felt: 'No human could be happier, nor have such a bursting soul.'

But almost immediately the mood changes: doubt and disquiet follow, sad self-questioning, a puzzled little cry to her mother across the void:

> I remain terribly childish and gawky in manner and speech. I like people but seem to have a weak form of communication or am simply rather an empty person.... Perhaps dancing is my best form of transmitting feeling. Life is strange.

The dancers loved Melbourne. Audiences were enthusiastic; they made many friends, being treated to parties and receptions and entertained in private homes in a most generous way. Their last performance was a tumult of shouting and flowers. Lynn had three curtain calls after her solo as Dawn in *Coppélia*, while afterwards a big crowd gathered around the stage door, cheering each of their favourites as they left the theatre.

They were very tired, not only from their heavy schedule of performances but also because of the great distances to be travelled by air and the rapid changes in temperature. She remembers one dreadful flight when the air pressure system failed. They all thought they were going to suffocate; several fainted or had to be revived with oxygen. Among those to faint was the brawniest and most aggressively masculine of the stage hands. This was afterwards a source of great amusement to Robert Helpmann, who would call out *'Oxygen!'* every time he noticed the unfortunate man climbing a ladder in the theatre.

After the triumph in Melbourne they travelled to Adelaide, a city which fascinated Lynn; to her it seemed quaint, almost like a stage set:

> It is terribly wild west with pillared wooden two-storied buildings with balconies. It only lacks hitching posts.

She went on several happy visits to a hillside farm where to her delight there was a menagerie of animals—retired cart-horses, a bandicoot, dozens of possums and an emu called Rose. She enclosed an emu feather and clippings with her letter. The farm, owned by Mary Clarke, a delightful sixty-year-old lady, very intelligent and much travelled with a passion for the arts and for animals, was Lynn's paradise; she has always loved individualists like her who 'do their own thing' which seemed to her the only thing worth doing, however much the cautious or the conventional might demur.

In Brisbane, tired of poor accommodation, she stayed in Lennon's, the best hotel in town and far too expensive for her. It was just as well. Next day terrible stories were told by 'the kids' of beetles, spiders and what she called 'cockroaches of enormous dimensions' in their rooms, to say nothing of mice, lolling insolently in corners. The heat was appalling, ranging

76

from 100 to an exhausting 114 degrees with high humidity. At her performance of *Swan Lake* she nearly collapsed at the end of the third act coda that contains the thirty-two *fouettés*, staggered to the wings unable to walk straight, so that she bumped into the proscenium and finally had to be pulled off stage by Helpmann and John Field.

A welcome respite was two weekends at the Surfers' Paradise on the coast, where she stayed as Helpmann's guest. It was a wonderful place to swim and relax, and Robert Helpmann's wit, kindness and fund of outrageous stories kept her and the other guests continually entertained.

Margot Fonteyn and Michael Somes joined the company for the last stages of the tour in New Zealand. This provided a welcome lifting of their jaded spirits, since by that time all the dancers were exhausted and longing for home. Lynn was greatly admired by the rather sedate New Zealand audiences, while the critical reception was perhaps the warmest of the whole tour. Dame Margot coached her in *Swan Lake*; it was, Lynn says, a marvellous experience: 'I was torn into little bits and ground into the floor.' That was just the way she liked to work.

The Company left by air for London after eight months away. They arrived on Wednesday 22nd April. Lynn slept solidly through the first day and night she was home. Her thoughts were dominated by the prospect of the future when she was to appear at Covent Garden for a single performance as a guest artist with the main company as Odette/Odile in *Swan Lake*. On that centred all her hopes. During the provincial tour that followed she lived for it, the dream that overshadowed her waking days.

# PART TWO

# 1: Soloist with the Royal Ballet

HE LONDON PERFORMANCE of *Swan Lake*, much longed for, much dreaded, took place on 6th May 1959. It went beautifully and was rewarded at the end with nine curtain calls and a cascade of flowers. The freshness of approach, the lyrical flow of movement in the second act and the real attempt to create a character out of the wicked Odile in Act III, rather than play her as an ill-natured trollop as is so frequently the case, indicated the workings of a rare imagination. Critics in London were enthusiastic; in Canada they went slightly mad. One writer coupled her and Antoinette Sibley as 'the girls who fight for Fonteyn's shoes'. Lynn was not pleased. Indeed she decided not to come home for a holiday that summer, as she could not face what she considered quite overblown publicity. She told her mother dryly: 'The performance was a certain kind of success.' In Vancouver, to her intense irritation, excited articles skidded off the presses. She had not, it seemed, just conquered Covent Garden; she had razed it to the ground. But that is where her feet were, very firmly; and she indicated that she was not amused.

Winifred Edwards put the matter in perspective. She wrote to Mrs Springbett:

> It was a very tentative first début and I hope there will be others as exciting and on a firmer foundation.... Lynn's entrance in Act II established her as an artist and a ballerina in appearance and figure. Her mime scenes were well played, her *pas de deux* beautifully danced and throughout her excellent musicality stood her in very good stead.

78

I deplore all the 'local' publicity—it is much too soon. Her talent is in its first buds—some unkind frost and it may not fulfil its promise. Play it down as much as you can.

It was a tremendous event in Vancouver, and rightly so. The mayor had telegraphed the city's best wishes. Lynn's parents gave her a beautiful pendant to mark the occasion—a gift more valuable to her than any rave review. Dame Margot's mother sent her a special message of congratulations.

After this début in *Swan Lake*, Lynn wrote to Fay Angus a letter that shows the calm professionalism with which she faced her career:

The performance at Covent Garden was one of those important points in one's career, but I have already forgotten about it. Indeed, the surface excitement had worn off by next morning. It does sound blasé and brutal but I refused in my mind to build up that particular performance any more than any other performance of *Swan Lake*.

There was not as much glamour in her life as the local press portrayed. For a time she lived in a vicarage off Kensington High Street, sharing a first-floor flat with the vicar's aged mother and her nurse. She had also begun, when on tour, to learn a new ballet, Andrée Howard's *La Belle Dame Sans Merci*, scheduled for the early part of a joint season by the two companies at Covent Garden in the summer. She played the lady, partnered by Donald MacLeary; there were also 'six knights [she reported] whom I have seduced'. She found Andrée Howard vague and difficult to work with; she hated the music, disliked much of the choreography that seemed to her remote and stylised, thus not being in accord with her present demand for dramatic realism in ballet.

A wonderful trip to St Tropez in June, with Kenneth MacMillan, Donald MacLeary and Lorna Mossford, used up two weeks of her holidays, but the second fortnight was spent taking classes from Kathleen Crofton, a favourite teacher of hers. To her great distress MacLeary was moved to the main company at Covent Garden: 'Svetlana has snaffled my beloved Donald.'

When she returned from holiday, she injured her foot

seriously in class and was not able to dance for several weeks, as a result of which she missed the first performance of *La Belle Dame Sans Merci* on 2nd September 1959. She went to it, however, 'dressed to the nines'. Slowly she began to recover, taking private lessons from Winifred Edwards, who had an uncanny knack of bringing injured dancers back to form. She was later to dance the role on tour, enjoying it more than she had during its composition.

Her friendship with Kenneth MacMillan continued to enrich her life. Their wonderful rapport when working together had grown into a genuine affection, both deep and constant with them both:

> Kenneth MacMillan was on tour with us and he is the one that's been making life worth while for me . . . He has an uncanny genius not only for his choreography but in points of production for individuals which is vital for a dancer and all too rarely received. He liked me—fancy someone liking me! I'm a sucker for anyone who pats my head!

The last two sentences are characteristic; the loneliness, the self-doubt and the longing to be loved are the three constant themes of her life. In this generous friendship that gave her so much and asked from her so little, they are drawn together and at least for a time resolved into a quiet harmony that brought a measure of peace to this anxious young dancer.

Soon she began to work with MacMillan on his new ballet, *Le Baiser de la Fée*, in which she had one of the most important roles—that of the Bride whose beloved is claimed by the Fairy. He had responded to the gentle lyricism of her dancing with choreography in a more romantic vein than any he had attempted before. Her attitude to the role, as she explained it to her mother, summarises exactly the central quality of her art: 'It is a matter of feeling truly about the story and identifying each tragedy and joy with one you have really felt.'

Early in the New Year the Company went to South Africa on tour but Lynn was told by Ninette de Valois to remain in London for intensive study of the classic roles, particularly Giselle. This gave her more time for thought and deliberation than she had been allowed in Australia, and her first performance in *Giselle*, at Covent Garden on 5th March 1960, showed far more the authority of the true ballerina, especially in the second act, than had been evident in her first, very immature *Swan Lake*. She had been deeply impressed by Ulanova's naturalistic approach to the role, somewhat to the detriment of her playing in the first act which lacked period style. She was, in fact, to abandon a great deal of this naturalism when she danced the ballet in future years.

Although the role does not contain quite so many demands on technique as *Swan Lake*, it requires a maturity of approach that is very rarely at the command of young dancers. In the first act she presented a delightfully child-like peasant girl, very simple and naïve—as one critic noted, it had 'a rather appealing gawkiness, like that of a foal'—but the tragic heroine of romantic art who should be discovered very early in the ballet was nowhere to be seen; far from being fated by a doomed love, whose intimations she could sense even from the first kiss, this was a normal, high-spirited child who, when betrayed, would have been more likely to box Albrecht's ears and go off arm in arm with Hilarion than to lapse into madness and death. The mad-scene had little conviction, which was strange from a dancer with such powerful dramatic gifts; but this may have been because the earlier interpretation had not prepared the way for it.

In the second act, the beautiful fluidity of her dancing, her exquisite floating arms that seem to drift on the slow tides of the music and her ability to dance the long *enchaînements* in one great sweep of movement, gave an extraordinary beauty to her performance, bringing a reminder of the ballets of long ago. It contained the majestic simplicity that is at the heart of the *danse d'école*, which Alexander Bland described as moments 'when she draws herself up like a tiny empress or langorously traces a liquid finger in the air'.

It was a clearer intimation even than *Swan Lake* that a rare ballerina was beginning to emerge and that de Valois' judgement of her potential was to be right. But it took her a long time to obtain the true feeling for the first act; the distance between nineteenth-century romanticism and modern dramatic ballet is very great and particularly difficult for a contemporary dancer to bridge. Nora Kaye, for example, who was the finest dramatic dancer of her time, was quite wrong as Giselle, making her so neurotic that it would have been better to send her to a psychiatrist than turn her into a Wili. Lynn Seymour, probably aware of this danger, made the

*Her first romantic role, that of the young bride in* Le Baiser de la Fée, *created by Kenneth MacMillan in 1960.*

famous mad scene stilted and unreal. She was later to suggest a Freudian interpretation of the character to Miss Edwards who observed that she would do better to seek for her 'in a Victorian album with lace-trimmed edges'.

Her performance as the Fiancée in *Le Baiser de la Fée*, first given at Covent Garden by the Touring Company on 12th April 1960, was greeted both by the public and the critics as a major advance in her career. An earlier version of the ballet had been created by Frederick Ashton as his first main role for Margot Fonteyn in 1935, so that it was very appropriate that one of her greatest successors should follow her. Only one critic had serious reservations about her performance, describing it as containing a surfeit of 'kittenish coyness with her girl-friends'. On seeing this in print, the irritated young dancer dismissed him in one word: 'Madman!' But the other critics were agreed: the gentle poetry of her dancing, with its dreamy flow, exactly caught the other-worldliness of the ballet, the air of enchantment and fairy tale.

As a result of this acclaim the press began to seek her out. An amusing interview in the *Evening Standard* opened with her saying that 'A little whisky's good for you', confessed her weakness for shoes and scent, and her consuming passion for ice cream. The interviewer caught one remark that is very typical of her at that time, with its amalgam of candour, self-mockery and lugubrious sense of humour:

> 'Being on the stage is torture the whole time. You can never be *absolutely* sure'—her eyes went wide in anticipated horror—'that you won't fall over and *sit down.*'

Lynn's studies of the great classical roles were bringing her in some terror to the most exacting of all: that of Aurora in *The Sleeping Beauty*. Any ballerina cast for the first time as Aurora had always the impossible ideal of Margot Fonteyn against which to judge her performance, since Fonteyn's interpretation was already legendary, one of the greatest enactments in modern times. Lynn danced it for the first time in Belfast in June. Now she was at last confronted by the *rose adagio*—with its terrifying balances *en attitude*, that supreme achievement of the classical dance—greatest of all test pieces for the ballerina where every flaw and deviation from the purest style is mercilessly revealed.

It was clear that the technical demands of this tremendous role sometimes exposed weaknesses, but she transcended these by the depth of her characterisation. Here was a young girl, eager and ardent, on the threshold of adult life, trembling on the brink of the awakening day, prefigured even in her name. It was a magical portrait, tender and yet with a hint of pathos, of a young princess leaving her childhood with wonder and a few regrets. No great distance separated this Princess from a modern young girl who takes her lover's hand as they walk down the street.

Christopher Gable, who could study her at close quarters during her performance, recalls how she transcended her technical limitations by this immersion in the role. The long balances of the *rose adagio* that have now sadly degenerated into a kind of acrobatic stunt, were not within her scope, but she dealt with this difficulty with remarkable skill.

'There was no way in which she could hold the balances *en attitude*,' Gable recalls, 'so she made a girl who had been very sheltered and was somehow put in the position of meeting possible suitors for the first time and they were extraordinary to her. I can still see the way she looked very carefully at the first one, and thought, "Goodness, you're nice," so, quite naturally with a young man, she held on to his hand. Then she came to the next, and she thought, "You're nice, too: I'm not sure you aren't even nicer." So she clung on again. Then to the third, and she said, "Why, I'm not sure you're not the nicest of them all." Suddenly, at the end, we had four men, not just four, but different men and a woman meeting them, so that the dancing became irrelevant or rather, relevant in a different kind of way.'

At this time she was beginning to work with Kenneth MacMillan on a new ballet, also about a young girl on the threshold of life; indeed, in certain respects, it was a modern and tragic retelling of *The Sleeping Beauty*, set in contrast to the fairy tale with the most cruel irony. Based on themes from two novels, *Le Blé en Herbe* by Colette and *House of the Angel* by Beatriz Guido, it is set in the Edwardian age, telling the story of the innocent growing love of two adolescents. The girl is raped by a middle-aged man, while the boy is seduced by his wife. The girl has lost her innocence and her hope; the idea of love has been destroyed in her forever so that when her young friend approaches her again, she rejects him. Kenneth MacMillan entitled his ballet, *The Invitation*. Lynn realised as they began to work on it that here was her great opportunity as a dramatic dancer. In the part of the young girl she could draw on the memories and feelings of her own life that had been enclosed within her for so long and extend them through her imagination.

Lynn had been invited home by the Vancouver Ballet Society to give two performances in July 1960. Christopher Gable agreed to come as her partner and she set about making the arrangements in so decisive a manner that she seemed to imitate Dame Ninette in the early days of the Vic-Wells Ballet.

Any deviations from the high standard of professionalism she had learned resulted in some well-placed rebukes that must have made the Ballet Society wonder at the change in Lynn Springbett. She was quite firm, polite but decisive in the best de Valois manner: there were to be no photographs taken during performances, no overblown publicity, Equity must be consulted, programme notes would be written by herself. She would decide the repertoire, brushing aside a timid request for one of the *pas de deux* from *Swan Lake* with the stern reminder that the Ballet Society must be aware that there is more to the art than the old, familiar classics. Two dressers must be found, rehearsal rooms provided; she must know the exact stage dimensions, and it would be quite improper and unprofessional for Christopher Gable to stay elsewhere than at an hotel. Overawed, The Ballet Society concurred at every point.

They were so proud of her though; her return was an event of civic proportions. She was met at Vancouver airport by the Mayor and his wife leading the official reception, then driven to the city hall. There she was presented with a special award of honour in the form of a gold-plated civic recognition medal and signed the visitors' book that included the names of Queen Elizabeth II, Prince Philip and Viscount Montgomery of Alamein. She was now Vancouver's tenth official citizen of merit. She looked pale but composed in a grey suit and a wide-brimmed hat; the Mayor was in his robes of office; the audience, comprising friends, local celebrities and members of the Ballet Society, was dressed to kill. The press noted that their new citizen of merit had gained a 'new-mint English accent'.

Her performances at the Queen Elizabeth Theatre on 27th and 28th June were announced in the press with quite a flourish: 'The Vancouver Ballet Society proudly presents Vancouver's own LYNN SEYMOUR, Ballerina Royal Ballet Company in her Canadian Première.' The house was packed to watch the local heroine. A company of thirty dancers had been engaged to support her, and there were in addition four ballets by Vancouver choreographers, including Nicolai

---

*The 'white'* pas de deux *in* Les Patineurs *partnered by Christopher Gable at a guest performance in Vancouver in 1960.*

*The lonely girl, the solitary one, in Kenneth MacMillan's* Solitaire.

*A* pas de deux *in* Solitaire *partnered by Christopher Gable.*

Svetlanoff. She and Christopher Gable danced three *pas de deux*: the 'white' duet, as it is known, from *Les Patineurs*, the *pas de deux* from *Solitaire* and *Don Quixote*, to end the evening with a virtuoso piece. Their success was enormous; bouquets thudded on the stage and the applause continued through many curtain calls.

It is, however, typical that Lynn never for a moment played the role of the great star returning in triumph. She stressed over and over again that she was not a ballerina, only a senior soloist with the touring group of the Royal Ballet; any talk of her as a successor to Dame Margot Fonteyn was brushed aside with visible impatience. Christopher Gable recalls that when she took class with the other dancers, nearly all amateurs, she worked in exactly the same manner as at the Royal Ballet School, not caring how many mistakes she made nor making any attempt to be different nor expecting preferential treatment. She was, like all the others, a working dancer; in no way was she a 'star'. Indeed, she has never cultivated a public image, nor played the expected role of a famous ballerina. She is too busy and too honest. Also she rather enjoyed then, as she does now, shocking the bourgeoisie: old tattered jeans, sagging sweaters and a slightly dishevelled look were more her style. She was delighted once to be described as 'a ban-the-bomb type' at the height of her sartorially hippy phase. At home, after all this glory, she enjoyed her holiday in simple, unaffected ways; then she was Lynn Springbett, who loved the beach, gigantic ice creams and being with mom.

When she returned to London, it was to a season with the Touring Company at Covent Garden, combined with commuting to Edinburgh for performances of *Le Baiser de la Fée* with the main group at the Festival. The first night there was nearly ruined when the scenery collapsed during the ballet, but by now she was used to such happenings after two years on tour. In London she danced the Polka in *Façade* for the first time, worried about the fast and very precise *pirouettes* that the choreography demands, and also appeared in Ashton's *Birthday Offering* in the variation created for Svetlana Beriosova. She had her troubles; during rehearsals at Covent Garden 'the Dame had a "Picking on Seymour day" so that I was in tears and ready to quit the organisation'. Dame Ninette felt it was good for young dancers with great talent to be savaged from time to time. Margot Fonteyn has recalled such moments in her autobiography, although 'Madam in a rage', while being one of Robert Helpmann's funniest party pieces and hugely enjoyed by the lady herself, was not quite as amusing at the time; indeed, it was inclined to produce a state bordering between extreme terror and the utmost perplexity, usually ending in tears and muttered imprecations in the dressing room, where letters of resignation were drafted and then, sadly, abandoned.

The main Company was shortly to begin another tour of the United States and Lynn was once more to be relegated to the provinces. However, as a bonus, she was to join them in New York for three performances in *Le Baiser de la Fée* at the Metropolitan Opera House in September 1960. Dame Ninette intended that one of the brightest new stars in her firmament should only be glimpsed for a few tantalising moments by the public and critics in the United States to which on a later tour she could return in triumph. It was an ingenious move, since this fleeting visit from a dancer who was in a sense a guest artist would draw attention to her; while only three performances would be remembered with more vividness than a dozen. Also, Dame Ninette felt that *Le Baiser de la Fée* was unthinkable without her. Lynn was her protégée, the great hope of the future; she would therefore insinuate her into the hearts of the wonderful American audiences Dame Ninette cherished so much and let a brief memory of her linger until she returned.

The whole idea worked beautifully: Lynn was a huge success, even if she was not satisfied with her own performance, since she was suffering from a bad attack of influenza which she had caught two days before. Dame Ninette was, however, so proud of her that she took no less a person than Martha Graham to see her dance, as she was quite certain that the great contemporary dancer and choreographer would respond to Lynn's marvellous musicality and sense of *plastique*. The response was unequivocal. When the curtain fell, Martha Graham turned to de Valois: 'It's not fair: she's got it all,' she said.

John Martin, the doyen of American critics, described her as 'a darling'. Another critic called her 'the most exciting young dancer to be seen in America since the emergence of our own native Allegra Kent in the New York City Ballet and the equally glorious Yekaterina Maximova of the Bolshoi Ballet'. The writer speaks of her in a memorable phrase, 'a divine wildness in the form', and continues 'She is a born and instinctive dancer and every phrase, gesture and movement is pure delight to watch. Obviously she is a national treasure. . . . It would be easy to fill an issue or book in her praise.' Dame Ninette must have felt that even from a critic who, by the nature of his profession, would be entirely ignorant of the art of ballet, this judgement showed some sense.

Lynn had, however, rather less patience with one of the other critics who kept referring either to her 'monkey-face' or, worse, to 'a face like a teacup'; it seemed rather ungallant, as well as being irrelevant to her work as a dancer. She had, in fact, an enchanting elfin prettiness, rather whimsical, her face lit by large seeking eyes, in a manner that was both demure and sensual. No wonder she was a little mortified to find herself compared to crockery.

The autumn and winter of 1960 were among the most demanding of her whole career. She was learning the role of

Ashton's Cinderella during their provincial tour; at the same time work on Kenneth MacMillan's new ballet, *The Invitation*, scheduled to be performed at Oxford on 10th November prior to its official opening at Covent Garden on 30th December, continued at fever-pitch. 'Ken is becoming a little more neurotic every day,' she reported to her mother with great satisfaction.

The dancers knew that the ballet would cause controversy and they worried about the reception in London, since the critics had been asked not to comment on the work until then. Lynn wrote to her mother:

> Kenneth has undoubtedly produced a master-piece—one of the most staggering works ever created and we all know it, but we also have a feeling that on its official press début in London it will be ill treated by the critics.

This season at Oxford was very important for Christopher Gable, since it was then that his great partnership with Lynn Seymour truly began. Ever since their first performance together as students in *Orpheus* at Cambridge they had developed a respect for one another's gifts as well as a genuine and lasting affection. Gable was not originally cast in the role of the young man in *The Invitation*; it had been given to Pirmin Trecu. However, Trecu damaged his knee and was obliged to withdraw; as a result of this Lynn suggested to Kenneth MacMillan that Gable should take over the part. He has never forgotten that it was through her intervention that both in this ballet and in *The Two Pigeons*, the one that followed, where again he was not in the original cast, she had been instrumental in giving him the two greatest opportunities of his dancing career. Over the next few years she was to owe as much to him; it was his innate sense of drama, his intuitive understanding of her inner life as an artist that was to draw from her those sublime dramatic interpretations upon which her fame has been built.

Her other new partner, since Beriosova had snaffled her divine Donald (MacCleary), was Desmond Doyle—a fine dancer and a handsome man with whom Lynn decided she was in love, although it was unfortunate that he was married. She had also that year developed a passion for the Danish dancer, Flemming Flindt, whose rather casual attitude to her admiration (of which he was entirely unaware) caused her some grief as well as a few hours waiting for the phone to ring. She described him to her mother as 'a hunk of Danish Delight'. For one with such a sweet tooth and a weakness for chocolates with soft centres there could be no higher praise.

At about the same time as she was troubled by these two newcomers into her affections, she had to admit she was casting envious glances at Dame Margot's new partner, a young Hungarian dancer, Viktor Róna, whose looks could only be described by her as 'pretty devastating'. She was in fact now dangerously susceptible, being drawn either to gentle, sensitive men with delicate feelings and inner doubts, or to aggressively confident types like 'the Danish Delight', who would dominate her and make her feel frail, feminine and defenceless. Problems arose when she demanded unavailingly that they should be both kinds of men either at the same time or at such intervals as her heart should determine, the choice of the day or the hour being at her discretion. Unfortunately such an ability to switch one's role is not a talent as easily acquired in life as on the stage and she was often disappointed, although she forgave them for not being what they could never be with all the sweet magnanimity of her nature.

At Christmas Lynn returned to Covent Garden to share the lead in Ashton's *Cinderella* with Margot Fonteyn, Nadia Nerina and Svetlana Beriosova. Her performance naturally lacked Dame Margot's polish and her wonderful attention to detail but it had a warmth, an innocence and a spontaneity, coupled with her quiet sense of fun, that brought new freshness to a role that is rather slim in the possibilities it offers a ballerina, although it is technically very difficult. Her stage manner, at once wistful, pathetic and eager, with its undercurrents of sly humour, suited the part to perfection; in many ways its lack of sophistication and high technical gloss made it more touching even than Fonteyn's, which was by now very much the interpretation of the *ballerina assoluta* rather than the downtrodden kitchen-girl.

The dancers had approached the Covent Garden season with great trepidation. They were sure they had a masterpiece to unveil with *The Invitation* but they also knew it might be either a scandal or an object of ridicule for both critics and public. Kenneth MacMillan had been obliged to change his original project for a work in two acts, as the composer,

Matyas Seiber, had been killed in a car accident before he could complete the score, and it had to be finished by one of his students. This tragedy made the dancers more determined than ever that the ballet should be a triumph. What they feared most was indifference. This drew them closer together and Lynn was no longer the prim, dull, little outsider to them; they were proud of her, even while they still mocked her a little for her alarming dedication. There is a charming glimpse of this in one of her letters to Carol Chambers:

> At the moment someone in the Company is sitting opposite me, sending me up and making writing impossible. Have just slugged him so life is now easier.

Like her friends in the company, she feared the worst: what she could not have imagined was that the first night of *The Invitation* was to make her famous. When this happened, she took it very calmly; but in her heart she was amazed.

# 2: A Choreographer's Muse

*L*YNN SEYMOUR woke on the eve of the New Year to find herself a celebrity. The reviewers, as she had hoped, went wild, not about the ballet, where they had many reservations concerning structure and dramatic development, but about her. Here they were unanimous; few young dancers have ever had such a press. It was ecstatic; the critics showered her with superlatives. And they were right: Lynn Seymour was tremendous. Her performance in *The Invitation* has now passed into legend, along with that of Renée Jeanmaire in *Carmen* and Nora Kaye in *Pillar of Fire*, as one of the greatest enactments of modern times.

Her playing encompassed a range of emotion that would have tested a dancer of great experience, let alone one who had only recently come to solo roles. The acting was achieved entirely through the body and the expressive force given to each movement, rather than through mime. Indeed, like Nora Kaye before her, Lynn has never been a notable actress in terms of facial expression, nor have any other of the great dramatic dancers. In *The Invitation* she managed to convey not only a whole spectrum of feeling—from innocence, shock, ardour, terror, to final repulsion and despair—but she was also able to show these in terms of a continuous development of mood, arising naturally out of the music and the dance. Many dancers can make an *arabesque* sing; only the greatest is able to convey anguish or terror within the formal limitations of the academic technique.

In the closing moments of the ballet, when the young girl takes on the movements of the frustrated governess of the earlier scenes, there was more than an imitation of certain steps and gestures; she gave us a personal insight, expressed in

95

her own way. This was not a generalised portrait of a young girl, one of the most frequent characters in ballets both classical and modern, but a certain girl, set at a particular moment in time and history. The sense of the Edwardian period was conveyed with extraordinary insight; this child was not the free young woman, Lynn Seymour, of her day. Perhaps the slightly narrow provincialism of her early life helped her to express a naïvety and innocence so appropriate to the ballet, particularly when one remembers how she was compared by Christopher Gable when he first her to a rather prim little Queen Victoria; nonetheless, her portrayal was an imaginative leap into new emotions, quite extraordinary in so young a dancer.

The work itself did meet a fair amount of criticism; it was considered over-elaborate, extended by too many incidents and unnecessary characters. In an amusing imaginary letter to Kenneth MacMillan, dealing with this point, Richard Buckle wrote of Lynn:

> By glancing in a certain way over her shoulder, then flinging off her hat, she could conjure up a whole regiment of governesses.

It was to be exactly the same when she danced in *Solitaire*, where one backward glance expressed a world of loneliness and inner doubt. It has always been her gift to people the stage with imaginary characters whom one can see through her eyes. So when she danced in *The Invitation*, she seemed to look beyond the present towards the adult world that awaited her, beyond the governesses and the statues, with their rather obvious symbolism, to the undiscovered land her heart was seeking. The essence of her performance is paralleled in some lines by George Seferis that convey the visionary quality of her dancing in the role, the wonder and awakening of childhood, the loneliness, the vision of those far imagined hills:

> *Our friends have gone*
> *perhaps we never saw them, perhaps*
> *We only met them at the time sleep still*
> *Was leading us close up to the breathing wave.*
> *Perhaps we look for them because we are looking for*
> *The other life that is beyond the statues.*

It is like this to be young, to see the future—'the breathing wave', as Colette saw it in *Le Blé en Herbe*, the novel that inspired this ballet. The exquisite, sensual delicacy of her writing was matched in the dance:

> Une célérité anguleuse et plaisante, un équilibre, exceptionnel comme un don chorégraphique, gouvernaient tous ses mouvements. . . . Malgré la force, chaque jour monstrueusement accrue, qui chassait hors d'eux peu à peu la confiance, la douceur, malgré l'amour qui changeait l'essence de leur tendresse comme l'eau colorée qu'elles boivent change la couleur des roses, ils oubliaient quelquefois leur amour.

If he had at first had doubts, because of the technical difficulties she experienced when they were creating *The Burrow*, Kenneth MacMillan had none now. As he said later:

> To work with her is like working with an extension of myself. We come to the same conclusions at the same moment. . . . She transcends the steps. She makes a role so real that you forget about the dancing. . . . She brings a sense of reality to an art that is very unrealistic. Quite simply, you believe her.

She believed in him, his view of life, the originality of his mind. Looking back over their work together she says:

> What's interesting about Kenneth's characters is that they're not run-of-the-mill people in the situations they're in. He has a wonderful sense of those strange dark areas of life. It's not straightforward bad or good.

Already she had come to know those dark areas—of loneliness and sudden depressions that came on her so stealthily. She relates them to those moods she found described by Herman Hesse as being 'under the wheel'. In one of her frank interviews she gaily told a startled reporter: 'I have a tough front, but it's all a front. I'm really neurotic. Yesterday I just decided to spend all day crying.'

*The Invitation* marked an important stage in Kenneth MacMillan's development as a choreographer. He recognized

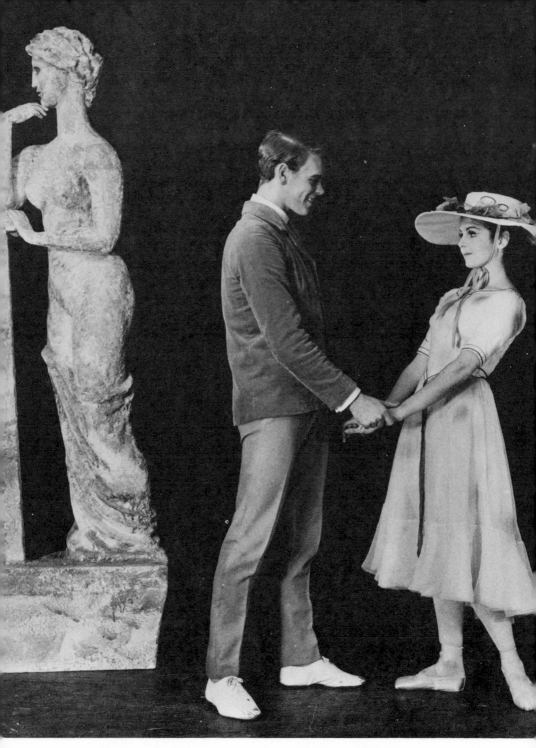

*Lynn's first triumph in* The Invitation *(1960) where the two young lovers meet by the statue; partnered by Christopher Gable.*

*The awakening of love in a* pas de deux *with Christopher Gable from*
The Invitation.

its importance to him, and failure would have been a shattering blow; in one of her letters Lynn says, 'I'm sure Kenneth will unhinge if it isn't a great success.' Now the success, if not complete, was enough to encourage him to venture further into the strange landscape of his art. He had set out the themes for his future development: the ballets of pure dance like *Danses Concertantes* with their wry, almost sardonic wit, in some ways both ironic and wilful; the works of mood such as *Solitaire*, holding within them a sense of loneliness, pathos and childlike wonder; the dramas of a dark, fantastic imagination like *House of Birds*, brooding with an almost gothic air of menace; and now the first of his great dance-dramas, *The Invitation*, where a complex of interrelated emotions is compressed into single *enchaînements* and *pas de deux*. It was on these foundations that the great span of his creative work was to be built.

Even as a young man Kenneth MacMillan was an explorer of a new range of feelings and Lynn Seymour inspired him to become a pioneer, one who has extended the boundaries of the formal dance further than any choreographer of modern times. This fact has been continuously ignored and MacMillan has been attacked, often with brutal insensitivity, for being a less fluent and refined choreographer of pure classical dancing than either Ashton or Balanchine, as if this were the central feature of his art. His true interest has, however, been elsewhere, set in the dark and troubled world of our unknown selves.

His themes are those of cruelty, ambiguous sexuality and searching self-doubt—an area of moral unease, often leading to fear and sometimes to madness, seen not only in terms of individuals but also of society itself. It is not by chance that the search for identity, explored in *Anastasia*, is one of his most obsessive themes; nor that insanity, sexual violence and the workings of a corrupt society, evident in such works as *Manon*, *Mayerling* and *Playground*, should draw his imagination so insistently.

This willingness to explore the more disturbing areas of experience is crucial to his artistic collaboration with Lynn Seymour. She has the same painful honesty about herself; as an artist she will not compromise with truth, even when it may show her in an unbecoming light. She is without artifice, either as a dancer or a person; no theatrical gloss, like that of some very famous artists, manicures her behaviour. Like MacMillan she is both stubborn and restless, in pursuit not of an airy vision but one of a harsh and often brutal reality about her own nature, to be faced equally unflinchingly in the dance.

She had the courage and integrity to follow him; together they agreed to search for truth, however dark or unpalatable both to themselves and the public, where it lay hidden.

MacMillan believes that Lynn's dramatic gifts are instinctive; they are a natural means of expression that do not have to be worked out in stages or intellectually, but arise from her own response to music. This, he thinks, has caused her much anxiety as she has no idea of the extraordinary impact her dancing makes on an audience and so becomes worried about real or imagined technical defects, not noticed by the audience who have been under the spell of the dramatic and emotional qualities of her dancing.

He does not accept that even in those early days she had great technical weaknesses, apart from the weak feet that had worried Dame Ninette. What she lacked was stamina, due to her physical build and her soft, extremely pliable body. She could execute any academic step or *enchaînement* with the same technical facility as her contemporaries, even dancers of considerable virtuosity like Antoinette Sibley, but what she could not do was to sustain the dance. This, MacMillan maintains, has been the source of so much criticism of her technique, which was an inhibiting factor in her early career and continued to worry her for many years. As Christopher Gable puts it in more colloquial terms: 'She just ran out of steam.'

What was presumed to be technical weakness was, in fact, a different approach to movement. This, MacMillan believes, is at the centre of her problems and of her relationship with the Royal Ballet. The Company had their ideal, one great international ballerina, the perfect example of what has become known as the English school. Quite rightly, Margot Fonteyn was the ideal set before every girl in the organisation: her fluidity of movement, her exquisite line and placing, her great musicality—all these were the vision they were seeking. This is as it should be: a large, classical ballet company must be led by a *prima ballerina* whose skill and authority place her far above her colleagues. But, as MacMillan points out, Lynn was and is a quite different kind of dancer—in training, in style and in outlook; most important of all, one with a quite different physical structure. She could never be a ballerina like Fonteyn; indeed she could never be a typical artist of the Royal Ballet. MacMillan considers she has been profoundly influenced by her early training in the Russian school by Svetlanoff. In a sense, he says, those in authority at the Royal Ballet, with the best of intentions, tried to 'cure' her of this, to make her more like a dancer of the English school, seeing (as Dame Ninette has pointed out) that her lack of good academic grounding was a serious limitation to her development as an artist. From this dichotomy doubts and hidden pressures arose within her; indeed, MacMillan believes that this unconscious rebellion expressed itself at one time in her unconventional manner of dressing and her jaunty defiance of the public image of the classical ballerina (of which Fonteyn was the supreme example), which was noted with much glee by journalists and gossip columnists. She resented being described as a 'second Fonteyn', partly because she recognised that Fonteyn was a great and unique artist, but also because she was the 'first Seymour'. And she was this sometimes to excess.

Although *The Invitation* was completed and successful, so that it has survived down the years, there are no endings in a dancer's life; there is only a new beginning, a new role, a different kind of exploration to be made. From the shuddering world of physical desire and the withdrawal from it in distaste, revulsion even, that is so much a part of *The Invitation* as it is in many of MacMillan's other ballets, she had to journey back into the past to the serene romanticism of Frederick Ashton's *The Two Pigeons*. Ashton had already warned her over lunch some months earlier that he was going to drive her to distraction, to punish her until she began to hate him; in fact, given his nature, no outcome could have been less likely. They worked together on *The Two Pigeons* in great harmony. For her it was so serene a world, with its pretty tuneful music by Messager—one of gentle sentiment, where a

*Lynn and Christopher Gable rehearsing for Sir Frederick Ashton's* The Two Pigeons *in 1961.*

young artist leaves his beloved for a gypsy girl, returns to her and is inevitably forgiven.

The ballet is a kind of game of love, wistful, evocative and childlike, in which—like the two pigeons that flutter across the stage at its close—the young lovers are sweetly reconciled. It is full of the imagery of fluttering wings, the strutting of pigeons, where the little beaten steps remind one of Valéry's delightful simile in which he compares a dancer's feet to two doves quarrelling over a patch of grain.

In the role of the young girl Lynn Seymour achieved a vast range of moods, for it is a ballet about moods and the changeable heart rather than a search for any emotional depths. She was by turns wilful, impetuous, stubborn, yielding, heartbroken and, with a certain reluctance and full of her memory of past hurts, at last sweetly forgiving. Christopher Gable who played opposite her, having replaced the injured Donald Britton in the main role recalls that at each performance she acted the part differently. There was a spontaneity and a daring that she had not showed before, indicating how much she had grown in confidence as a result of her triumph in *The Invitation*. She was both maddening and lovable, spoilt and generous, unpredictable and constant; indeed she was herself—her many selves that her friends had come both to love and to despair over.

She has always enjoyed *The Two Pigeons*, although like many other dancers in the role she has sometimes had trouble with the white pigeons who have important parts in the ballet, especially at its close when they are supposed to flutter across stage to join the reunited lovers. On one night, she recalls, one of them decided to take a turn or so round the auditorium, then joined the dancers for their final *pas de deux* and took a curtain call with them, digging its claws into her neck.

It might have seemed that after a series of brilliant successes, crammed into a few hectic months, her career would surge upwards on a crest of mounting triumphs. But it was not so. Indeed, the two years that followed the first performance of *The Two Pigeons* on 14th February 1961 contained almost continual disappointments and a series of cruel misfortunes.

---

Previous page: *The young lovers are finally reconciled at the close of* The Two Pigeons: *Lynn and Christopher Gable.*

And her career has always been like this. She has known the heights and the depths, and they have come too swiftly one after the other; what she has rarely achieved is a long period of slow, steady progress in which she could develop, as was the good fortune of Margot Fonteyn before her. She has never been long enough on the peaks to view her kingdom; instead she has suddenly been forced to gaze back at them from the depths of the dark valley.

There is possibly a certain element of self-destruction in her temperament, as there is in that of most artists; but circumstances have played against her—continual injuries, problems with her weight, the pressure of domestic or financial difficulties, all these have not been self-induced. The will to succeed is so strong, passionate even, but not for fame or wealth or high living (although she is not averse to any of these things), that success seems to appear unfulfilling if it has not been achieved after a great struggle; if it came too easily some part of herself had to invent greater obstacles to block her progress. In an interview she makes this observation: 'I like to feel pain like that. That kind of pain is accomplishment.' She would, one suspects, prefer to fail after a tremendous struggle rather than succeed after no struggle at all.

John Gale, who was to become such a close friend until his death in 1974, paints a remarkable portrait of Lynn at this time in his posthumous novel, *Camera Man*, in which the heroine, Belinda, is clearly modelled on her—although fact and fiction are inextricably mixed. Here this curious ambiguity in her nature comes out very clearly:

> She had made an impression on him from the very first; there was always, strongly, *something there*: something that he would never forget: it was not only bravery, wildness, a tendency to self-destruction: it was a quality deep and untouchable.

But grief lay in the future, after the triumphant nights, the cheers and the falling flowers. Now it was marvellous: she had entered into her inheritance as the foremost dramatic ballerina of her age. She was so proud of the ring Nora Kaye had given her after *The Invitation*: it came from the greatest dramatic ballerina of the previous generation.

In March she went for a weekend to Paris with her friend

*A* pas de quatre *improvised on a flight to Tokyo, with,* (left to right), *Doreen Wells, Anya Linden, Beryl Grey and Lynn.*

---

Donald MacLeary in response to an invitation from Flemming Flindt, 'the Danish Delight', who was dancing at the Opéra and confirmed that it would be 'an agreeable duty' to show her the city. She adored the Left Bank, was suitably shocked by the transvestites in the 'Carousel', where she and Donald danced what she modestly described as 'a sensational cha-cha'. They also went to see Flemming Flindt in *Swan Lake* at the Opéra. Lynn was not impressed by the production; indeed, she was horrified. 'You've never seen anything so terrible in your life!' she gasped to her mother, with a battery of exclamation marks to indicate each separate gasp. She was also not greatly enchanted by the fact that Flemming Flindt's girl friend was also in Paris.

As she was so often away on tour, she gladly accepted Donald MacLeary's invitation to take a room in his flat for the brief periods during which she was in London. This shocked her mother, who had to be told that her friendship with Donald MacLeary was beautiful and chaste—as indeed it was. Like all very feminine women she had many close and warm friendships with men whom she loved in a far less acquisitive manner than those women who are unsure of their powers to attract. This did not prevent her from eyeing others with a certain, rather less detached interest.

A tour with the Royal Ballet to Tokyo, Hong Kong and Manila followed in May. She loved the season in Japan, being delighted by the extraordinary courtesy and consideration of the Japanese, the enthusiasm of the audiences and the splendid hospitality lavished upon the dancers. The first performance at the Tokyo Metropolitan Festival Hall was attended by the Crown Prince Akihito and Princess Michiko, Princess Chichibu, together with the Foreign Minister and members of the Government. She was fascinated to visit the *Takarazuka* theatre, a feminine version of the *Kabuki*, where the women are brought up from childhood as performers. The performances were so long that Lynn and other members of the company had to take a packed lunch with them.

The dressing rooms had been altered for the Royal Ballet dancers, as these were designed for tiny performers; even the smallest member of the company felt something of a giant in this miniature world. Lynn visited the night clubs, some of them definitely sleazy, accompanied by her friend, Anya Linden. Together they stayed in an old inn in Kyoto, the ancient capital of Japan, in an atmosphere that recalled the vanished Imperial world.

In Hong Kong they had to travel by boat to reach the theatre, which was set in a squalid part of town. Here she rebelled when she found she had to share a room with three other girls and moved to what she describes as 'a Humphrey Bogart type of hotel with shutters'. It was vastly more expensive, to the horror of the promoter who was forced to foot the bill.

At Manila the Company was lavishly entertained by the Philippine Dance Company, who took them on a tour of the jungle villages. Lynn remembers the houses on stilts, where one could see the interiors as if they had been sliced in half. They travelled in airy buses with no windows; watched a cock-fight at a place called Tai-by-Tai, and visited a crater at the top of a volcanic mountain. At the end of the season they were entertained at a party of quite astounding lavishness, returning home by air the next day, many of them a little queasy after so many exotic dishes.

In August she was on tour again, working on her technique

over many performances of *Don Quixote*. 'I have been trying to become a virtuoso dancer,' she remarked, dead-pan, in a letter, adding in huge capitals: 'BIG DEAL!' Their tour to Baalbeck, Damascus and Athens in late August and September 1961 came as an enchanting interlude. The company danced at the open-air Temple of Bacchus in Baalbeck, where it was so hot that they had to begin rehearsals very early in the morning and finish by midday. The dancers wore sun hats to rehearse, David Blair being splendidly dressed in the headdress of an Arab sheikh. George Issa who was Dame Margot's driver became quite devoted to Lynn; when the company returned to England he was to write (via a professional letter-writer) copious letters to her, full of local news and professions of an undying friendship. The stage in front of the Temple was so vast that to traverse it in the *grands jetés* of *Les Sylphides* meant that Lynn had to leap more like a gazelle than a sylph. But the setting was perfect—the illuminated temple behind the stage, where bats flickered through the evening air. Fokine's reverie could never have been set in a more haunting perspective.

They drove in a cavalcade of cars from Baalbeck to Damascus through a desolate and frightening landscape. The frontier guards were particularly unfriendly; the dancers had their passports checked while they looked down the muzzle of a gun. Here they danced in a tent, wired for electricity in a somewhat haphazard manner, so that if you happened to touch a bulb or wire an alarming electric shock followed. There were nervous yelps from the dancers as they crowded the wings waiting for their entry.

After this, the winter tour of digs and dull towns, where a dirty rain seemed always to be falling, was not a happy contrast. By now Lynn had enough of touring and she told Dame Ninette so. Dame Ninette had, however, the last word—this being the one she likes to reserve for herself—and told her that her promotion to the Covent Garden company was to begin on 1st January of the next year. Having thus achieved what she wanted, Lynn perversely began to doubt whether she wanted it at all, for she would lose her great roles (such as in *The Invitation*) with the Touring Company and have far fewer performances. It was not that she was unreasonable, but ... it had been, after a glorious beginning, such an empty, dreadful year. She looked to 1962 with a more guarded enthusiasm.

110

Over the past year a happy relationship had been developing between herself and Colin Jones, a dancer—not a very good one—in the Touring Company who planned a different career as a photographer. He was neither 'a hunk' nor a kindred spirit, but a gentle, sensitive young man whom she could trust and whose companionship was increasingly precious to her. One of the most pleasant happenings of what was soon to become a detestable year was that he obtained a job as a photographer with the *Observer* and quickly began to make a name for himself.

Then ill luck struck again with choreographic precision. The privincial tour ended in November and Lynn was due to dance her first London performance of *The Sleeping Beauty* a few days later on 11th November. She was obliged to cancel this owing to a strained achilles tendon. At first this did not seem too serious, but it became inflamed and nearly five months were to pass before she was able to appear again on the stage. She nearly despaired; without her dancing she was 'a deaf-mute with sounds and words building up in me fit to explode'.

Her only consolation was that after a lot of searching, in February she found a basement flat in Pimlico's Aldeney Street, a dingy road which she described as being 'very convenient', presumably because there was no bus stop or tube station within easy reach. She loved the flat, the basement of John Cranko's house which had been divided since he was now in Stuttgart. It was her first real home—a suitable place for her Japanese prints, the pride of her small collection. Colin Jones helped her to decorate. Otherwise she was miserable. In February she was knocked down by a car and had to stay in bed for a few days. 'What else can happen to me now?' she lamented, gloomily awaiting the worst as she gazed up through the railings at the tramping of anonymous feet.

Winifred Edwards was as ever her salvation—'dear, darling, wonderful Miss Edwards!' She had a genius for restoring injured dancers to the stage; indeed, this painful interlude was of great value to Lynn, since it gave Miss Edwards a chance to take her technique apart and rebuild it from its foundations. 'The whole thing,' Lynn was to say later, 'gave me a second chance at the technique I've lusted after so terribly.' But it was a bad time, the first six months of a year being followed by a number of accidents and injuries that effectively kept her from main roles with the Company for some twelve months, with

spasmodic returns in small solo roles, followed by further painful relapses and once more a slow rebuilding by the imperturbable Winifred Edwards.

After a bad six months full of accidents and unsuccessful performances, she rejoined the Touring Company in August. Because of her injuries, the plan for her to be with the main company at Covent Garden had to be postponed, so that once again she faced provincial theatres and all their hazards. At one of these, a converted cinema, she recalls that there was no way of passing either behind or under the stage, so that she had to wait during the whole of the third act of *The Sleeping Beauty*, pressed against a brick wall in the non-existent wings.

In October she travelled with the Touring Company to Hamburg, West Berlin and Copenhagen, as a break before the winter tour. In November came the first real brightening of the year, when she began to work with Kenneth MacMillan on his new ballet, *Symphony*, to music by Shostakovich. It was during this tour that she told her parents that she and Colin planned to get married. Although such a modern, outspoken young woman, she was a very dutiful daughter and wrote in a formal way to seek their approval. At this stage in her life she was a rather provincial, straight-laced girl from overseas, still somewhat proper and conventional; while from this cocoon was slowly emerging the brilliant, witty and somewhat disrespectful maverick, who cared little for her public image as a great figure in the ballet world. In fact she was to go a little to the other extreme—not just jeans and a sweater, but very old, torn jeans and a jumper that one witty reporter described as looking 'like a hand-knitted lobster-pot'.

Her parents, of course, approved, although in a cautious way, since Colin's career was in its early stages and Lynn, even though she was now a senior artist with the Royal Ballet, earned a ridiculously small salary. A definite date for the wedding was not fixed but Lynn hoped that a return visit to Vancouver as a guest artist with the Ballet Society in the following summer could be combined very well and economically with her wedding. To obtain such a happy conjunction of events, she would not be quite so authoritative

---

*As Princess Aurora in the first act of* The Sleeping Beauty *in 1963.*

about what she was to dance—that is, of course, within limits. It was also by now almost certain that she would be with the Royal Ballet on a three-month tour of the United States and Canada, when the dates for a July wedding and guest performance in Vancouver would coincide exactly. Maybe the sullen gods would smile on her at last, but looking up from her beloved basement flat to the sullen winter skies, she rather doubted it.

# 3: In the Shadows

ℐT MUST HAVE SEEMED inevitable, like being run over again. Now, having learned Kenneth MacMillan's new ballet, *Symphony*, she developed influenza just prior to the first night on 15th February 1963 and had to withdraw from the leading role. Even for someone so stoical in temperament it did seem a bit much, since a change of fortune was badly overdue. She allowed herself, as she had done so often in childhood, a good howl.

The ballet particularly was important for her, since working on it with MacMillan had brought them so close together as artists who shared an almost telepathic rapport. *Symphony* had been an exhausting struggle for him; never had she known him search for so long and with such difficulty for images that seemed continually to elude him. It seems to her now like the agonizing gestation of a new phase of his art that was to be triumphantly affirmed in the *Song of the Earth*, created for the Stuttgart Ballet two years later. Not only did she observe this painful rebirth but she worked with a fierce intensity to help him release his imagination from its chains. However, his art still remains a mystery to her. As she says looking back on those days:

> Where his talent comes from, I don't know. We are inextricably together as soon as we begin to work, each knows what the other is about. It's uncanny.

His admiration for her as an artist, his love for her as a person continued to amaze her; the old question she had asked five years earlier, when he first chose her from the *corps de ballet* to dance in *The Burrow*, still nagged at her mind—'Why me?' she asked herself. 'Why me?'

Her friends formed a small enclosed group, affectionately referred to by Sir Frederick Ashton as 'The Diners' Club'. Apart from Lynn and Kenneth MacMillan they included the designer Nicholas Georgiadis, whose majestic sets for *Romeo and Juliet* lay in the future, Kenneth Rowell, Donald MacLeary, Peter Darrell and Jeffrey Solomons who was not a dancer, a designer or a choreographer but a most amiable and intelligent man. Peter Williams, now the editor of the magazine *Dance and Dancers* and a distinguished critic of the ballet, often joined the group, advising them about performances and lending them books from his large collection. Others came and went but this was the nucleus.

They were, Lynn remembers, 'like a group of Rockers wandering around London'. They met to discuss every subject under the sun—literature, films, the theatre, arts, politics; surprisingly not so often the ballet—and they entertained each other at their different homes on a kind of loose rota system, meeting up for tea each Sunday as a more or less fixed arrangement. As Lynn recalls: 'I suddenly had a family, not only sweet and loving, but also hugely interesting. It changed my whole life.'

But the trail of misfortunes seemed endless; several years later, in 1968, she was to write of this time as

> ... the accumulation of all the blackest, hardest and severest agonies of my life. . . . But that's over and my heart and soul are free of the worst, although they cast a shadowy memory.

It did not make her cynical, as this is not part of her nature, but a sense of gloomy fatalism took its place—a method by which she sought to steel herself against misfortune. The only thing that gave her cause to smile was the role of the Tango Dancer in Ashton's *Façade* at a gala performance at Covent Garden in February, when she was partnered by her beloved Robert Helpmann, the greatest of all exponents of that famous dance-hall gigolo, beringed, glossy and steeped in oily self-satisfaction, his eyes flashing in manic glee. They brought the house down; to see her adjust a smile like a slipped hem, in an attitude of outraged gentility when her partner suddenly up-ended her was a memory to be cherished for many years. Winifred Edwards describes her performance as one of 'a real, zany little deb'; and while that is true, there was also a faint air of musty provincialism about this little dancer who so bravely tried to match her worldly partner grin for grin, being at the same time dreadfully uncertain of her assumed sophistication so that her smile had a way of skidding alarmingly in moments of woeful self-doubt.

When she was able to take over the main role in *Symphony*, danced by Antoinette Sibley on the first night, one could see immediately that the creative relationship between herself and Kenneth MacMillan had developed further. The ballet carried traces of *Solitaire* which, although created for Margaret Hill, became in time Lynn Seymour's signature work. Once again she is a dancer apart from the others, lost and lonely, a child in a world she only half comprehends but in which she suffers half knowingly, like a child.

The Company left for another tour of the United States in April, opening at the Metropolitan Opera House, New York, with *The Sleeping Beauty* on 7th April. The tour lasted twelve exhausting weeks; from New York they travelled to Baltimore, Philadelphia, Boston, Detroit, Toronto, Chicago, Seattle, Portland, Los Angeles, ending with a series of performances in the Hollywood Bowl.

In New York she stayed with Nora Kaye and her husband Herbert Ross. When they had to leave for Europe on a business trip, she remained on at the flat, looked after by Nora Kaye's 'darling mom'. She achieved a great critical and public success in her début in *The Two Pigeons*, one writer describing her 'glowing warmth and markedly individual style that heighten and colour every phrase she dances'. The ballet was not, however, a success with the public, so that after the New York engagement only the first scene of the second act (the gipsy scene) was danced, thus leaving her without a role in it. She did, however, give what she describes as 'a couple of tortuous performances in *Swan Lake*'. She was much admired in *Symphony* and in *The Invitation*; several critics commented on her individuality, so different from that of the other ballerinas in the Company.

Colin joined her in New York together with Kenneth MacMillan, travelling out together on 'The France'. The tour ended on 7th July, when she went on to Vancouver where she had arranged guest appearances for the Ballet Society to be followed by her wedding. 'This is where I really belong,' she said on arrival in Vancouver. 'The air smells wonderful and I want to get used to it again.' She wore her big, floppy hat to celebrate the occasion.

On 12th and 13th July she danced at the Queen Elizabeth Theatre with Desmond Doyle—the Tango from *Façade*, the great duet from Act II of *Swan Lake*, a section from *Solitaire* and the last act *pas de deux* from *The Sleeping Beauty*. The bill was completed by a performance of *Les Sylphides* and new ballets by Vancouver choreographers, Grace Macdonald, Mara McBirney and Kay Armstrong, all featuring local dancers. Flowers cascaded on to the stage, and the audience cheered her with a special warmth—their favourite daughter had come home to be married. The wedding took place on 16th July; it was a civil ceremony, followed by a reception at the Vancouver Yacht Club. They spent their honeymoon inland, far away from all the publicity which Lynn so detested when she came home.

Whatever doubts her parents might have had about the marriage (neither Lynn nor Colin was financially secure and Colin was only beginning his new career as a photographer), they were greatly reassured by a letter from Winifred Edwards. No one understood Lynn's fears and uncertainties better than she, for no one knew her better. She wrote to Mrs Springbett prior to the wedding:

> How excited and half-pleased, half-apprehensive you must be over Lynn's forthcoming marriage. I think my main feeling is one of great gladness for her. I believe the loving companionship and security of marriage will give her what she has lacked so much through all these years. . . . I think they will start life together as comrades, on a level with each other, give and take. But Lynn will no longer have to wear the armour these children build who are proud, reserved and lonely.

When they returned to London for the next season at Covent Garden, Lynn and her husband had a new home, which had formerly belonged to her dear friend Anya Linden who had married (as Lynn puts it) 'a sweet millionaire'. It was a large, four-roomed flat in Charleville Road, very close to the Royal Ballet School; it was a rather run-down area, but Lynn assured her mother that it was coming up in the world,

118

though slowly. They began to decorate at once, aided by friends, but they never seemed to make much progress with all the big rooms; eighteen months later they were still hard at it. Furniture they accumulated slowly—a dining room table made from a friend's front door and a nice kitchen chair of which Lynn was rather proud as she had found it in the street.

Lynn returned to the role of Aurora for the first time after two years, when on tour with the Company at Wolverhampton. At Covent Garden she appeared in *Symphony*, *La Fête Etrange*, *The Invitation* and *The Two Pigeons*. At this time she was also getting to know Rudolf Nureyev, though neither of them could realise how deeply they were to care for one another in the years that followed. She asked him to dinner, confiding to her mother that he was 'a sweet boy, but very confused'. She had, however, to admit that such a state was not unknown to herself either.

She made a half-hour documentary film called *Telescope* for CBC, directed by Alan King, and transmitted the following January; in other respects it was a quiet beginning to the season. The main event lay in the future when the Company was to present a series of three ballets to celebrate the fourth centenary of Shakespeare's birth. Frederick Ashton was to mount *The Dream*, based on *A Midsummer Night's Dream*, Robert Helpmann to revive his celebrated ballet, *Hamlet*, first performed by himself and Margot Fonteyn in 1942, while MacMillan was to compose a new work, *Images of Love*, built round quotations from the plays and sonnets. Lynn would appear in *Hamlet* as Ophelia, the role created by Fonteyn, opposite Nureyev in the title role, and also in Kenneth MacMillan's ballet. Work started on this programme late in the year, while the routine series of performances continued at Covent Garden. Christmas was marvellous: the young couple entertained Colin's parents at a family dinner in their own home, the occasion being marred a fraction as all the lights fused. 'Very embarrassing,' Lynn told her mother.

In February 1964 Lynn travelled to Stuttgart to begin learning the role of Juliet in John Cranko's version of Prokofiev's ballet; she was taught by Marcia Haydée, her old friend from the Royal Ballet School days, now *prima ballerina* of the Stuttgart company and the inspiration for Cranko's finest works. They shared the same physical problems and also an innate

dramatic sense that was to make them in many ways so similar as artists. Lynn loved to work at Stuttgart. The dancers there were full of welcome (not a very frequent experience for guest artists) and she grew to love them dearly—'the fabulous kids' as she described them, so open in their generosity both to her and to their audiences.

John Cranko, through the extraordinary warmth and richness of his personality, had created in a few years a group of young artists totally dedicated to their work and profoundly committed to one another. Lynn found the atmosphere wonderfully exhilarating. It was agreed she would return in May to dance in *Romeo and Juliet*, partnered by a fine dancer from the American Ballet Theatre, Ray Barra, during a festival week of ballet.

The first performance of the Royal Ballet's Shakespearean evening was given at Covent Garden on 2nd April 1964. Rudolf Nureyev danced the lead in *Hamlet*, having been taught the role by Christopher Gable, who had himself learned it from Helpmann. Lynn was perfectly cast as Ophelia, catching both the moods of innocence, heartbreak and madness with a beautiful understated effect that she had not always been able to achieve in other ballets. It is a work of great power and theatrical imagination in which she and Nureyev—dancers in many ways so similar with their fierce inner conviction in the role they are playing—matched one another superbly.

MacMillan's *Images of Love* was not so successful, since he did not succeed in integrating dances based on a selection of quotations from the plays and sonnets into a meaningful whole. As in all his works it showed moments of extraordinary insight, images that seemed to shape themselves around the poetic line, but the general effect was scrappy and formless. Lynn appeared in a *pas de deux* with Christopher Gable based on the line, '*If you love her you cannot see her*', and in a trio (where they were joined by Nureyev) composed on '*Two loves I have of comfort and despair*', in which Lynn as the Dark Lady is torn between the poet and the fair angel in an erotic, intertwined

*The trio from Kenneth MacMillan's* Images of Love *in 1964, created to mark the centenary of Shakespeare's birth, with Rudolf Nureyev and Christopher Gable.*

trio where she had the chance to smoulder darkly, treating the poet with cool viciousness that seems to be fully in accord with the lady herself, now that Dr Rowse has found her for us after four centuries of hiding within the sonnets. When the ballet was taken on the next tour of the United States, some of the dancers heard a member of the audience call it 'Images of Lovely', and afterwards it was always so described.

Her one performance in Stuttgart of *Romeo and Juliet* was a huge success. It was her first major guest appearance abroad and Peter Wright, who at that time was Ballet Master at Stuttgart, remembers how she was almost paralysed with nerves before the ballet commenced; yet she danced with the freedom and authority of a fully experienced ballerina, winning the hearts of both dancers and audience. There was one alarming mishap during the third act, when the shoulder strap of her costume broke. Her partner, Ray Barra, danced the whole of the bedroom *pas de deux* with her, trying to prevent the costume from slipping to the ground. When she left the stage she was met with a battery of ladies from the wardrobe, their mouths full of pins, who quickly repaired her dress in time for her to visit Friar Laurence's cell. She rose from her knees, having received the good Friar's blessing, only to find he was standing on her dress which disintegrated once more.

After the Stuttgart début she travelled from there to join the Royal Ballet in Munich, where *The Invitation* was greeted with such enthusiasm by the first night audience that in the end she had to take her final calls through the door in the safety curtain. German audiences have always responded to her dancing; its sweep of movement and sense of *plastique* are qualities much admired by them, for Germany has a great tradition in the modern dance, a tradition that goes back to the times of Mary Wigman, Rudolf Laben and Kurt Jooss, pioneers of the Central European school of dancing, many of whose concepts are carried forward in her style and approach.

Another guest appearance for her and Christopher Gable was with the Marseilles Ballet in their production of *Giselle*. Both dancers brought their own costumes but the management was insistent that they should wear those provided; these, Lynn considered, were ugly and unsuitable. Protracted negotiations ended in deadlock. Finally the French Director of the company relented, as they were otherwise such charming and helpful guests, but with such reluctance that Lynn and Christopher kept their costumes locked in their hotel rooms in case of further hostilities. Christopher Gable remembers that when he went to a bar across the road during the height of the dispute, he found most of the resident company settled down in two distinct groups with a void of empty tables between them. The two factions, he discovered, were those in favour of Lynn's criticisms and those against; between them an angry silence lay. It took him a considerable time to make peace, so that rehearsals could continue in a less chilly, though hardly sociable manner.

Her partnership with Christopher Gable was the happiest and most creative of her whole career. She says: 'I lost fear on the stage because he was there. After him it became a much lonelier and much more frightening event.' They were for him too the richest years spent in the ballet, since dancing with her had suddenly opened up for him a world of dramatic truth that until then he had not believed was the province of the dance at all.

The Royal Ballet's summer season was at Drury Lane. Here she returned to *Giselle* and danced for the first time the Lilac Fairy in *The Sleeping Beauty*. A gala performance at Covent Garden gave her a chance to perform the famous duet for the Can-Can dancers from Massine's *La Boutique Fantasque*, partnered by Alexander Grant. She was a very earthy doll, sensual and not a little coarse, closer to Lautrec's *La Goulue* than any of her predecessors in the role. This, one realised, was a tough, hard-bitten professional who belonged to the cabaret and the sleazy music hall which, one suspects, is not quite what Massine intended. Lynn's most famous predecessor in the role, Alexandra Danilova, had stressed its elegance and sophistication, but Lynn is not interested in fantasy and sophisticated contrast, she is interested in life as she knows it and as her audience lives it. If this is the great strength of her dancing, it can betray her in works that are purely those of artifice. It is interesting to recall that even as a child she was far from impressed by the Massine ballets she first saw at Covent Garden, to the extent that she was harshly critical of the management for presenting them; his world of grotesque fantasy, a vision of a cartoonist or clown, is for her too remote from the truths of life that she has always sought to express in her art.

During the Royal Ballet season at Drury Lane she received an urgent call asking her to take over from Margot Fonteyn the ballerina role in a *divertissement* from *La Sylphide*, arranged by Erik Bruhn at the Bath Festival. The assassination attempt on Dame Margot's husband, Roberto Arias, that has left him paralysed ever since, had just taken place. Lynn learned the part in one afternoon; then after an evening performance at Drury Lane, she travelled overnight to Bath to dance at both the matinée and evening performance, returning next day for the revival of *The Two Pigeons* in London.

Almost immediately after these rushed series of engagements she travelled to Amsterdam to join the company in two performances of *The Invitation*. It was one of the busiest periods of her career, so that it is not surprising that the decorating of the flat was not progressing very fast. Only one room seemed to be done to any satisfaction, the main reason being that she and her husband—to say nothing of innumerable visitors—were tired of stepping over packing cases and oddments the whole time; it really became essential to make a clear passage between cans of paint, boxes and pictures still to be hung on unpainted walls, into which nails had at least been hammered in approximately the right places.

At the end of the Drury Lane Season she and Colin fled to Ibiza on holiday, where they stayed at the little village of Santa Eulalia. They were joined by Christopher Gable and his dancer wife, Carol. They were reported by the police for bathing in the nude and were chased for a considerable distance by the *guardia civile*, but they escaped without detection. It was the sort of holiday Lynn enjoyed.

In September she and Gable took part in a televison programme for CBC in Toronto, where they performed the *pas de deux* from Act II of *Swan Lake*, their duet from *Images of Love* and the balcony scene from MacMillan's *Romeo and Juliet*. This was the first section of the ballet he was creating, and so was danced five months before the full-length ballet was seen at Covent Garden. Rudolph Nureyev, who had been delighted by her performance in *La Sylphide* in Bath, recommended her to his friend, Erik Bruhn, who was mounting a production for the Canadian National Ballet. The performance took place at the O'Keefe Centre in Toronto on New Year's Eve. Erik Bruhn was taken ill and replaced at very short notice by Rudolf

Nureyev. The three of them worked in great harmony on the production; as Lynn wrote to her mother: 'We've become very very good friends—a sort of fan club for each other.'

Throughout she was marvellously aided by Rudolf Nureyev as her partner and their ever-deepening friendship is one of the most enriching experiences of her life. Although they differ in many ways in their ideas about the nature of the dance, each understands and loves the intense professionalism of their approach to their art. They share a common love of taking risks, a certain wildness, lack of discretion and fake gentility. She and Nureyev do not care about appearances; they care for their art, rather than their image: above all they care for one another in a gentle, loving way. Their colleagues sometimes find them impossible; this surprises them a little as they are only being themselves, and that only occasionally to excess. Each speaks very much to the point, and this has sometimes been the point of no return for other, less direct persons.

Two extremely vulnerable people, sometimes aggressive towards the press or to intruders if they feel that vulnerability threatened, they have found much in common both in their natures and in their art. He respects and loves her daring, her passionate commitment to the role, her tough no-nonsense attitude in a world so ingrown and prone to poseurs and vapid theatricalism. Above all, it is his profound understanding of the expressive nature of ballet that has been a continuing inspiration to her. From him she has learned and she has allowed herself to be guided by him with artistic humility. Other than Dame Margot Fonteyn, there is no ballerina he treats with greater patience and consideration, guiding her with the most touching concern. Fellow dancers have remarked that were she to fall flat on her face, he would be likely to congratulate her on making a most imaginative addition to the choreography. In her private life, which has contained more than the usual amount of difficulties, he has helped her in a way that has been a source of great happiness to her. Lynn recalls:

> Nureyev says that the only thing in life that will never betray you is your art. And there has never been anybody more faithful to this, to his mistress as it were, than he. Maybe I should take this as more of

a lesson, as I think I have betrayed it from time to time, wanting to enjoy all the other things of life.

Again she says of him:

> I love his total honesty about his work, honest in a way I've never seen before. He would put himself through the wringer to do it correctly. He'll even sacrifice perhaps a theatrical moment to do it the way it should be done. He has immense integrity, really down to the bone. I'll never forget his belief in me, his trust, even during the worst sort of times.

What Nureyev loves about Lynn is this same honesty and commitment; as he put it during these early days of their friendship:

> She is the most promising of all the young dancers in the world today. When I dance with her, I'm dancing with a woman. Even on a bare rehearsal stage she gives out a kind of magic.

Nureyev's impassioned romanticism in the part of James inspired Lynn to give a tremendous performance. Despite the fact that he had an injured ankle, as a result of slipping on the icy street, he danced with seeming ease; between them they shared nineteen curtain calls. He had learned the role in two days.

Some of the critics were not kind to her; curiously, in Canada she has often received more chilling notices than in Europe, as if some critics resent the fact that she returns to them as a guest rather than dances with them as a native. Ballet in Canada is in certain quarters very chauvinistic. One writer, however, described her 'decorous abandon' in the role, and this could not be expressed better.

On a lighter note, Lynn recalls a party given in Toronto where she met the famous Danish dancer, Frank Schaufuss. His son, Peter, a curly-headed boy of about fourteen, was there with him and he solemnly invited Lynn to dance with him, an invitation she accepted with some condescension, little knowing that this boy was to become one of the greatest and most admired dancers in the western world.

The year had indeed ended on a high note and she was justifiably happy. The terrible period that had preceded it,

126

wrecked by injuries and sickness, was behind her; ahead lay the role of a lifetime—that of Juliet in Kenneth MacMillan's version of *Romeo and Juliet* that was scheduled for next year at Covent Garden. She wrote to her mother: 'I've got madly, marvellously slim and everyone is thrilled and my rivals are worried'.

As well they might be.

# 4: Restless Juliet

*L*YNN RETURNED FROM Canada more determined than ever to decimate the critics; the snide remarks in one newspaper had angered her more than she pretended to her mother when she said 'We have some even worse ones in England.' She reverts to the theme a little later:

> I've come back full of fight and ready to set the world on fire with my *Romeo and Juliet.* If ever there was a role for me, it's this one.

She and Christopher Gable worked with furious intensity as the first performance in February 1965 approached. They studied the play line by line, testing each sentence to see what could be wrung from it, either in emphasis or gesture; and they spent long hours wrestling with details of interpretation. Sometimes in the middle of the night when an idea occurred to her often relating to some problem left unresolved during rehearsals, she would ring him to discuss it. Neither Lynn's husband nor Christopher's wife made more than token protests, even when the conversations went on into the small hours of the morning.

The making of the ballet was among the most creative experiences of her whole life; between herself, MacMillan and Gable there grew a kind of intuitive understanding of the music, so that phrase after phrase of the dance seemed to grow from it almost unwilled—particularly in the great *pas de deux,*

---

*A* pas de deux *from a later revival of Kenneth MacMillan's* Romeo and Juliet, *partnered by David Wall in the role created by Christopher Gable.*

*The final scene in the tomb from MacMillan's* Romeo and Juliet *with David Wall as Romeo.*

which have a fluidity, a lengthening of the poetic line in movement and an intensity of imagery that MacMillan had never previously encompassed in choreography.

Often in the past he had created startlingly original movement, full of emotional undertones of the most subtle kind, but here in the *pas de deux* he achieved a sense of flow that is an organic growth from one image to the next, so that one is not conscious of any joins or small linking steps needed to bind an *enchaînement* together. In no other work did the shape of the dance seem to grow out of her body; the movements were a kind of extension of herself, marvellously idealized, in

which the soft curves and blurred liquidity of her dancing were caught up in his invention as if she had drawn them on the air.

Lynn Seymour's body has always been his inspiration; her sense of line is so individual, not the icy perfection of the great classicist, but something that melts and flows and extends itself in heroic sweeps of movement. It was all these things he discovered in the great *pas de deux*, especially in the balcony scene. Often in rehearsal he asks the impossible of her; she has remarked wryly that he still expects her knee to bend the opposite way to normal, yet it is when she cannot do the impossible that her attempt produces something new, something impossibly beautiful.

*Romeo and Juliet* is one of those rare creations that always

131

enclose their creator within them, whoever dances the role later. Other such works are the magical solo Ashton created for Markova in *Les Rendezvous*, the leading part for Margot Fonteyn in *Ondine* and Petit's *Carmen* for Jeanmaire. Other dancers will do wonderful things with them, like Natalia Makarova as Juliet, but they are songs that belong to one voice. It is ironic, therefore, that the first performance of *Romeo and Juliet* was not danced by Lynn Seymour and Christopher Gable, where the roles breathed with their beings—her abandonment and divine wildness of spirit, his ardent and impetuous entrance into the dance—but by Margot Fonteyn and Rudolf Nureyev, great artists but not MacMillan's chosen ideals. This was because the management of the Royal Ballet felt it was essential that new major roles should be provided for Fonteyn and Nureyev for the forthcoming tour of the United States, since it was their reputation and vast popularity that ensured the success of the visit.

On the first night, 9th February, Fonteyn and Nureyev achieved a great triumph; it was a masterly interpretation of Shakespeare's play but it was a little distanced from MacMillan's vision, as audiences on 18th February discovered when Lynn Seymour and Christopher Gable entered into their inheritance. This is not to say they were better in the roles, but they seemed more at home in them, as if they had been brought up in the narrow streets of Verona, hearing under their windows the clash of swords and the music caught in the soft airs of a Southern night that breathe through the score with such throbbing insistence. The press was ecstatic; not since the first performance of *The Invitation* four years previously had she known such acclaim. The passionate sweep of her dancing; its fierce dramatic intensity, as moving in the great duets as in the moment when she sits alone and motionless on the bed in a trance of anguish; the sense of total abandonment to love and to grief—all these were her own. The part is hers and no ballerina, however great, can ever escape this beautiful ghost who will forever haunt the ballet.

It would not be unfair to Kenneth MacMillan to say that his Juliet is as much his own view of Lynn Seymour as Shakespeare's view of his heroine. In her performance Margot Fonteyn was perhaps closer to the text, where Juliet, although a young girl caught up in a violent passion, is not as dominating and tempestuous as MacMillan envisaged. In the ballet the action is, to a large extent, determined by Juliet, who is more headstrong and impetuous than her lover; there is a wildness in her, an abandonment to physical sensation that is more modern in concept than the first hesitant response of a virginal, unawakened child of the Renaissance. MacMillan's Juliet would cry out with all the passion of her blood:

> Spread thy close curtain, love-performing night,
> That runaways' eyes may wink, and Romeo
> Leap to these arms, untalk'd of and unseen.
> Lovers can see to do their amorous rites
> By their own beauties; or, if love be blind,
> It best agrees with night.

But there is also the frightened Juliet, who still clings to her childhood, who doubts the beating of hot blood:

> I have no joy of this contract tonight:
> It is too rash, too unadvised, too sudden,
> Too like the lightning, which doth cease to be
> Ere one can say 'It lightens.' Sweet, good night!
> This bud of love, by summer's ripening breath,
> May prove a beauteous flower when next we meet.

Lynn Seymour is not by nature circumspect. She is, both as an artist and a human being, not one to prevaricate, to hesitate, to weigh the consequences of impetuous action; and it seems that it was this 'wildness' in her, the workings of a fierce will, that MacMillan gave to his Juliet. The critic Richard Buckle got nearer to the truth of her interpretation than anyone else when he wrote: 'Seymour is odd, modern, original, touching and perfect.' He also speculated that, during rehearsals for *Romeo and Juliet*, he could well imagine Lynn suggesting: 'Could I chew gum during the balcony scene?'

This describes one aspect of her interpretation, for she was a modern girl in love, transported to the streets of old Verona. She was immediate (her double might have been sitting beside one in the theatre) but she also belonged to a different time and a distant age. Lynn Seymour had transferred the Kings Road to Verona to make us aware of the two worlds at the same time.

Once again, of course, the usual clamour about 'a second

Fonteyn' began—something that acutely irritates her. She realizes that such attitudes are naïve in the extreme: there will never be a second Fonteyn, any more than there will be a second Ulanova or Makarova; the greatest artists are unique and even immortal. The long-vanished shade of Carlotta Grisi still seems to haunt a moonlit corner of *Giselle*, just as the ghost of Nijinski lives on in Petroushka's cell from which neither time nor fading memory will ever exorcise him. The ballet is full of bright, immortal ghosts.

No sooner had the clamour over *Romeo and Juliet* subsided—in which ballet-goers were involved in some pretty rough in-fighting to agree the respective merits of the four ballerinas who played Juliet during this time—than the Company was off again on a long tour of the United States and Canada. They were to open at the Metropolitan Opera House in New York on 21st April, ending the tour with a week at the Queen Elizabeth Theatre in Vancouver from 20th to 25th July. This would be the first time Lynn had returned to her home town as a recognised ballerina with the Royal Ballet.

Lynn danced the second performance of *Romeo and Juliet* in New York, meeting the same critical acclaim as in London, even though she had the ordeal of following a first night danced by the idolised Fonteyn and Nureyev. She and Gable received no less than twenty-two curtain calls, an unprecedented number on a second night. One of the most experienced New York critics, Walter Terry, wrote:

> Miss Seymour and Mr Gable brought a quite wonderful lyricism which, with its lilting overtones, made the two seem like teenaged lovers.

Mr Terry could not resist also reporting the fact that Friar Laurence was wearing a glittering wrist-watch.

The critic of the *New York Times*, the most influential paper in the United States, was unequivocal:

> It is possible to say that Miss Seymour and Mr Gable did project subtleties and qualities in the work that Dame Margot and Mr Nureyev did not reveal.
>
> Miss Seymour was a special delight. Her youthful appearance and manner seemed made to order for the part of Juliet, and the impetuousness of her

responses to Romeo, as well as her depiction of the transformation of Juliet from girl to young woman, were utterly convincing.

She and Christopher Gable were described in *Vogue* as:

> The darling, terrible children—with time-lapse glimpses of a modern high school girl and a college junior—of Kenneth MacMillan's version of the Prokofiev ballet. Lynn Seymour sizzles with deceptive dramatic force: she can imply puppy fat. Christopher Gable, revved-up, powerful, has excited a young gaggle of fans. Neither dancer fills a balletic cliché. They simply break hearts.

The American press found her a delightful interviewee, even though the management waited anxiously for one of her famed indiscretions; what seemed to appeal to them most was her passion for ice cream and Shostakovich, to which more references seem to have been made than her gifts as a ballerina. Asked about her future, she considered that she would like to spend it 'beachcombing on a coral island, like Humphrey Bogart'. The reporters could not get to the telephones quickly enough. Frederick Ashton, who had taken over the directorship of the Royal Ballet from Dame Ninette in 1963, would smile his inscrutable smile and say nothing; in fact, being under great pressure himself, he might well have thought it a good idea.

Big classical ballet companies, contrary to popular belief, thrive on one or two mavericks within them, although it is difficult to be an individualist in a large group. While Dame Ninette herself might rage and shout, flinging her stick, jumper and anything else within range far across the studio, she had a very soft spot for those she categorised as 'little devils'; in many ways, even in her mature years as a world-famous artist, Lynn Seymour still enjoys bouts of non-conformity, when she is as pliable as milled steel. The Americans adored her for it, just as they adored the impassioned intensity of her dancing, symbol of her impetuous, wayward heart.

No less delighted with her was the impresario, Sol Hurok, a man of outsized personality, charm and business acumen, who had made and lost fortunes promoting ballet and for whom the dancers of the Royal Ballet had become his dream children after years of disillusionment with the art and its performers. He really adored Lynn because she was so pretty, outspoken and down to earth, without any of the theatrical langours that in the past had driven him to distraction with other great ladies of the ballet. If Margot Fonteyn was his goddess and the greatest dancer he had ever known, Lynn was his accompanying cherub. 'Never mind about her being a great actress in ballet,' he said. 'She would be a great actress in drama and would make a big name for herself in straight parts.' Christopher Gable, her favourite partner who understands her better than most people, agrees; but he can never tempt her on to the stage because of her anxiety—like nearly all dancers—that her voice has neither the range nor the strength to cope with the theatre. It is rare for a dancer to continue in the theatre as an actress or an actor after their dancing career has finished: the great Lopokova tried, as did Moira Shearer, neither with much success. But Christopher Gable has succeeded and is now a considerable actor with a growing reputation. The many-sided Sir Robert Helpmann is perhaps the exception: half dancer, half actor or, as John Field puts it, 'a hundred per cent dancer and a hundred per cent actor'.

The tour followed much the same route as in previous years, with engagements in Philadelphia, Washington, Baltimore, Boston, Toronto, Chicago and Los Angeles as the main centres. They danced from 1st to 6th June in the Place des Arts in Montreal, where the Canadian audiences welcomed the return of their fellow countrywoman with immense delight.

In Toronto she was partnered by Rudolf Nureyev in *Giselle*, and one reviewer described her performance as one 'of transcendent power and atmosphere'. In San Francisco a critic speaks of:

> . . . the utter beauty of her dancing, a romantic-dramatic emotion that gathered rapture, intensity and overwhelming tragic spirit as the story proceeded. Her dancing had a silken creamy flow, whether slow or swift. She was tenderly lyrical. She was brilliant with the utmost refinement.

Certainly this critic did rather disgrace herself by describing her figure as 'chunky'; at this period in her career it was most unfair, since the recurrent weight problem (because she was happy) did not affect her at all. Of course Lynn never improves matters much in this way when she talks to the press, being the type of person who jokes about what worries her most; she told one interviewer 'I am eight stone and when that comes flying at you it's quite a lump.'

Remarks like that did not help at all, any more than this: 'You should have steel wire in the middle of you somewhere. I haven't. I have something more like sponge rubber.'

The Company made sure that when the tour made its final stop in Vancouver Lynn was to dance at practically every performance. She appeared in *Romeo and Juliet* on the second night, 21st July, in *The Invitation*, and closed with a performance of Odette/Odile in *Swan Lake*. After this performance the whole theatre rose to her.

During this tour her friendship with Rudolf Nureyev was a constant source of happiness, as they seemed to have so much in common. They even had the same misfortune of being insomniacs; often in their hotel they would talk on the house telephone, discussing every subject imaginable for hours through the night. By day he would carry her hat for her.

Immediately the season ended in Vancouver, Lynn joined the Canadian National Ballet for a season in Washington, dancing with them for the first time as a guest artist in *Solitaire* and *La Sylphide*. There was no break for her at all; the Vancouver season ended on 25th June, whereupon she travelled direct to Washington, arriving the next day for rehearsals. Two thousand five hundred people crammed into the vast open-air Carter-Barron amphitheatre for the performance which was attended by the late Hubert Humphrey, then vice-president of the United States. *Solitaire* was warmly received, with thunder and lightning joining the applause, and her own performance was recognised as one of the most remarkable of modern times. No dancer has ever caught the mood of wistful pathos, the eagerness and disappointment of a lonely child to such perfection.

Lynn attended a reception at the White House but the dancers were less than enchanted when each was presented with a ball-point pen when they left. The tour of North America, following so soon upon her triumph in *Romeo and Juliet*, marked the high point in her career; maybe she alone knew of the shadows that were beginning to gather round the edges of her happiness. At the end of the season there was her holiday, where she joined her brother Bruce and his wife at Lake Tahoe in the United States. They bathed and lay in the sun; they laughed; it should have been perfect.

Then the new winter season at Covent Garden was in preparation and with it the sense that she was resuming her old life after the adventures in the United States and Canada. She visited a specialist about the weight problem, again a matter for anxiety. He was able to reassure her that this was due to the under-functioning of the thyroid gland, which made her feel that it could be controlled and understood. In fact, as she had already suspected, the condition was exacerbated by mental factors; it could not be cured as easily as she then hoped. And she faced a crisis in her personal life as painful as any she had previously known. By now her marriage was showing signs of deep conflict, however desperately she and Colin tried to resolve their incompatibilities. It was such a difficult marriage to keep secure: she was an established, international star, recognised as one of the greatest young dancers in the western world; he was a photographer, making slow and difficult beginnings in a new career.

Their work often separated them and he must have unconsciously resented the fact that she was a huge success in a career in which he had failed. Her single-minded dedication to her future, now opening up to unimagined horizons as a result of her triumph in *Romeo and Juliet*, created a difficult imbalance in marriage that people who were far more experienced and worldly might have found hard to resolve. Money was a continual problem as neither was well off and both were extravagant. Her fame had brought her in contact with a large number of people in the arts—poets, writers, actors, painters—with whom Colin found little in common. She was developing as a person, eager to learn, to make new discoveries in art and life; in marriage she found herself constricted, and their quarrels became harder and harder to reconcile. Between them there was not bitterness, so much as a sad but growing recognition that the relationship could not be sustained. Their problem was a distressingly familiar one. An artist as fully committed as Lynn works in her own particular solitude. The dance was her language—at that time the only one she fully knew. Later she was to make decisions, accepting in advance their consequences for good or ill, and never demanded any refund in lost happiness. But she was young when her marriage broke up, and she could not understand.

The strain was intolerable; her weight inevitably began to cause difficulties. Finally, for the first time, her indomitable spirit cracked. She had a nervous collapse brought about both by physical weakness due to the deficiency in the thyroid and mental stress. A letter to her mother, written in October, tells this in all the sad, graphic terms so well known to those who have suffered the same agonising condition:

> I retired for a week—a sort of snivelling mess. It's funny how suddenly one has no more fight, determination, ego … just an empty collapsible hulk of flesh. . . . I couldn't even go down the road to buy a pint of milk without the most extreme anxiety, and had to come back without. . . . Whether I can gather myself now I don't know. . . . Perhaps I'll be able to go to work tomorrow without dying or being revolted by myself. I've lost all desire to work or do anything. I've no confidence, no self-love.

Somehow, with psychiatric help, she managed to drag herself back to work, although the old enthusiasm had gone. She danced by memory, the sheer force of her professionalism, but the freshness and vividness of her interpretations were lost. The Company travelled to Rome and Milan, where she had a huge success in *Romeo and Juliet* with Christopher Gable, whose friendship was such a support to her. Then the London season opened on 16th November. A month later she and Colin agreed to separate. She left her home to stay with Nigel Gosling, the art critic, and his wife, Maude Lloyd, a former dancer of Ballet Rambert (under the pseudonym 'Alexander Bland' they have written ballet reviews for *The Observer* since 1952). They treated her with great gentleness, leaving her alone when she wished, never interfering, but discussing her problems with her whenever she needed comfort. She wrote a brief, sad letter to inform her mother. They had parted, she said: 'With no bitterness or hatred: just a rather aching sadness and a feeling of isolation.'

On the day she and Colin decided to separate, Lynn visited

Winifred Edwards to whom she had turned for comfort for all her problems, from those of a child trying to stitch her ballet shoes to those of a young woman suddenly lost and alone in a world filled with terrible imaginings and aching memory. She was comforted, as she knew she would be; more than that, she began to recover her belief in herself as an artist. Winifred Edwards knew that only there could her peace of mind be recovered and her life achieve the same harmony that was founded in her dance.

Lynn wrote to her mother in January, a little restored after a New Year's holiday with her beloved friends, 'the dreamy kids' of the Stuttgart Ballet:

> Miss Edwards has been magnificent and ever since my breakdown in October has been giving me a lesson daily, free of charge, also so many other kindnesses, too many to mention, and much basic good sense and understanding.

The pattern of her career had again repeated itself: from triumph to grief. But a new road now opened for her. And she had the courage to follow it.

# 5: The Willing Exile

*I*T WAS TIME for a change. After such a shattering crisis Lynn felt she could not resume her life with the Royal Ballet at Covent Garden and on tour as if nothing had happened. She was sometimes dancing less than a single performance a week at the very time when she knew that her fullest potential as an artist could at last be reached. Having made the decision with Colin that their marriage was at an end she felt a huge sense of relief and liberation. She wrote to her mother early in January 1966:

> Happily, there is no remorse, no blame and nobody else involved, and now it's a time of unencumbered rethinking and sorting out, like convalescing from a long illness. One feels slightly delicate, but all things have a new look and a new taste and meaning.

But she was discontented and restless at Covent Garden, despite the warmth and friendship from many of her colleagues there—notably Svetlana Beriosova and Georgina Parkinson, who had shown her many kindnesses over the years and were to continue to do so. Her huge and devoted public continued their clamorous support at each performance, but she had reached a dead end. Only one new ballet was in preparation, a revival of John Cranko's *Card Game* which he had created for the Stuttgart Company; neither Frederick Ashton, his creativity sadly limited by the responsibilities of directing the Company, nor Kenneth MacMillan had new roles in mind for her. There was in the Company a feeling of marking time after the excitement of the last American tour, one of their most successful ever; they had passed the creative peak that had gone into the making of

*Romeo and Juliet* and had involved many of them in important roles. She wrote to her mother:

> Actually, my time with the company has not been very good either, but even if things improve to my benefit I still feel it won't be fulfilling enough. It's so large and has so many fabulous dancers, so few performances and such an unchanging policy . . . that I feel my last years will be wasted and frustrating. I am quite aware that one's years as a dancer are very short and I feel that while the wish and passion is there it should be indulged. It's safe here, but the pioneer blood is strong in me and makes for unruly discipline, and passionate action.

An unusual challenge for her was to appear in a television drama *Albertine*, based on the play *Le Rideau Crimoisé*, that combined both dancers and actors. The choreography, much of which took place in bed, was by Kenneth MacMillan and the production by Peter Wright. The story is a simple one: a man dies while making love and his mistress has to move the body from her parents' bedroom to her own without being discovered. Peter Wright remembers how beautiful Lynn looked on the screen; some of the shots—particularly in close-up—were exquisite, catching the expression of her wide, luminous eyes. He believes that with her intense feel for dramatic movement, her unusual beauty and emotional intensity, she could have become a great film actress. She also took part in the television programme *Tempo*, in which her opposite entertainer was Tom Jones, whom she was to describe to her mother as 'dreamy'.

The first performance of *Card Game* took place on 18th February, with Christopher Gable in the grotesque leading role of The Joker. Lynn had a small part as the Two of Diamonds in the 'Third Deal'—a gorgeous, zany little figure, the odd one out in a suit, a sort of comic version of the girl in *Solitaire*, making valiant and on the whole unsuccessful efforts to join her companions. She looked like a limp rag doll, all arms and uncontrolled legs, flinging herself at the others and usually missing them completely; at one magnificent moment she treads across their prostrate bodies like a cat on hot bricks, her eyes wild and horror-struck. Her gift for surrealist comedy—a gift that Robbins was later to discover in *The*

*Concert*—was marvellously exploited. At times she was almost frantic with misplaced enthusiasm, wiggling like a fish in and out of Stravinsky's edgy music, mouth agape.

But this was not enough and it was then that her great chance came. Kenneth MacMillan was offered the appointment of artistic director of the Deutsche Oper Ballet in Berlin early in May. It was a company that had fallen on hard times, its last two ballet evenings having been dismissed by the German critics as 'a scandal'. This was exactly what MacMillan needed to revive his creative impulse, now somewhat frustrated at Covent Garden. He is a deeply sensitive man, and his treatment by both critics and public over the years had not, with honourable exceptions, been very fair; his work, so daring in its exploration of the darker reaches of human emotion, was misunderstood and he needed freedom to experiment on a wider scale. As a result of his contacts with the Stuttgart Ballet he realised that it might be possible for him to achieve the same results as John Cranko, one of his closest friends and mentors, and he was eager to take the risk. Sir Frederick Ashton did not attempt to dissuade him; like Dame Ninette he has always been anxious that his young artists should spread their wings, and no one understood better the anguish of frustrated talent. But MacMillan needed Lynn. Without his muse, his chances of creating new, experimental work would be limited. Rumours in the press proliferated, but it was late summer before her decision to join him in Berlin was confirmed.

In the light of subsequent events it might seem now that she acted unwisely; indeed, it would have been more prudent to wait a year or so to see how the company in Berlin developed. As a result of her triumph in *Romeo and Juliet* she was riding the crest of a wave, even if the past year had been a lean one in terms of new roles and wider opportunities.

There were also those who saw it as a form of desertion, and when she returned from Berlin to the Royal Ballet she was not greeted with enthusiasm by all the dancers. Some of them felt that they had borne the heat and burden of the day only to lose important performances to her.

All her life she had made, both in artistic and personal affairs, such decisions with an impetuosity that is so much part of her nature. And maybe—even without the gift of hindsight—she has sometimes been unwise. Dame Ninette de

*The three pioneers off to Berlin in 1966: Lynn, Kenneth MacMillan* (left) *and the designer, Barry Kay, seen shortly before the first performance of* Anastasia *in 1967, for which Barry Kay created the décor.*

Valois, who understands her so well and loves her so much, thinks this may be the case. As she says:

> I know many artists of great intelligence and creativity, but it does not always go with wisdom. Wisdom is a very difficult thing to define; it is something quite different from a quality of intellect. You can find real wisdom in a woman like Lilian Baylis. She was as wise as an old peasant who looks out at the sky and tells you what it is going to do next month. She often said: 'I'm an ignorant old woman, my dear, but I always know who knows.' That remark showed her natural wisdom.

Impulsiveness, wilfulness, impetuosity: whatever word one uses, it is—and will always be—one of Lynn's abiding characteristics. It has made her a tremendous dancer with a range, a freedom and a daring beyond that of nearly all her contemporaries, but in terms of human suffering she has paid a high price. Perhaps this is but one aspect of the hard bargain

144

life makes with those who are the most gifted. As Alfred Adler wrote about Dostoievsky:

> Whoever holds within his breast such contrasts and is forced to bridge them has to delve deeply to find a resting point. He will be spared no trouble, none of the sufferings of life. He cannot pass the most insignificant creature without testing its formula. His whole nature compels him towards a unified interpretation of life, so as to find security and rest from his eternal wavering, his doubts, his unrest. He has to discover truth in order to find peace.

In April she had been to Stuttgart to see Kenneth MacMillan's fine new ballet, *Song of the Earth*, which he had created for them in 1965. Lynn recognised it at once as one of his greatest works. Here he reached a point beyond the exploration of human relationships, which Fokine and later Tudor had pioneered in the classical dance, to express concepts about the meaning of life and death that are contained in Mahler's music. MacMillan's sense of the transitory nature of human life, seen as a brief preparation for death, which is to be accepted in a mood of quiet resignation, is displayed in a choreographic argument of continuous growth. The ballet is a structure of great daring, where formal elaboration passes into classic simplicity so that the final statement in the trio is enclosed within a single image that contains all that has previously been so intricately shaped. Again Seferis best expresses the truth of those closing moments:

> *We who set out upon this pilgrimage*
> *Looked at the broken statues*
> *We forgot ourselves and said that life*
> *Is not so easily annihilated;*
> *That death has ways that are uncharted*
> *And a justice that is its own.*

While in Stuttgart Lynn danced a little solo from *Napoli* during a gala evening, then went straight on to Vienna to appear in Rudolf Nureyev's production of *Swan Lake*. She learned his new version of the choreography—in many ways very different from that at Covent Garden—in five days, dancing two performances on 15th and 25th April. She then joined the Touring Company for a performance of *Swan Lake* in Oslo before returning to London to learn the role created by Marcia Haydée in *Song of the Earth*. Haydée danced as a guest artist for the first two performances at Covent Garden in May and then Lynn took over the role.

Marcia Haydée is the most difficult of all dancers to follow in a role created for her. As Lynn points out, her strong back and the extreme flexibility of her achilles tendon allow her to perform the very fast spins, with both feet together, her body crouched low, that are a feature of the choreography and perfectly designed for her but for no one else. She is able to hover above the music like a hawk about to fall on its prey; and this quality MacMillan was able to exploit in *Las Hermanas*, another role which Lynn Seymour found very exacting. A further problem with *Song of the Earth* is that the mood of self-pity, that Lynn sensed both in the music and the dance in the last scene, is one to which she has always found it difficult to relate. Few vices are more obnoxious to her, both in herself and others, and this has caused her some inner resistance to what she sees as the emotional heart of the music.

If Lynn is never fully at ease in roles created for Marcia Haydée, the same thing works in reverse. This gives one a startling insight into the range of Kenneth MacMillan's creative imagination. He can make roles for two different ballerinas which, in emotional as well as technical terms, present them with huge problems when these are shared. It indicates, too, his understanding of the temperament and expressive range of two artists from whom he can demand different qualities, as much spiritual as technical, knowing what is the potential within each of them. This, of course, affects the style and content of his ballets created for them; as he says, 'If *Requiem* or *Song of the Earth* had been created for Lynn Seymour, they would have been quite different ballets.'

The greatest dancers, particularly those with strong personalities, can create where needed a sense of distance between themselves and their audience; against their natures even, they can be remote and solitary as lost stars. Lynn Seymour achieved this in *Song of the Earth*. In the wonderful final scene she was alone with the music, isolated from us all, like the protagonist of John Heath-Stubbs' poem:

> *Desiring never lover's touch, but only*
> *Abstract caress of song, and that cold flame*

*That sweeps around you, flickering, springing from*
*The dancing rhythms of your own clear blood.*

In May she was able to tell her parents that she had definitely accepted the offer to join Macmillan in Berlin as his ballerina. He intended to reinforce the company by several additions— Ray Barra, a fine dancer from the Stuttgart Company, was to join as ballet master and Vergie Derman, a South African girl, then a soloist with the Royal Ballet—tall, fair and beautiful, exactly the type of dancer for whom MacMillan liked to create—was to accompany Lynn. The New Zealand conductor, Ashley Lawrence, was also to join them from Covent Garden as musical director, together with the Australian designer, Barry Kay. This little group of artists from the Commonwealth, none of whom spoke the language, was his advance party. Not surprisingly the German dancers, already in occupation, received them with some caution. If they were not going to stand the Oper Ballet on its head, at least they were all quite determined to put it on its feet.

It was a huge challenge, something Lynn has always adored. If she cannot find a brick wall to beat her head against, she will build one as rapidly as possible; and the stolid, bureaucratic, opera-dedicated organisation in Berlin could not be a larger or less easily conquered fortification. So, the small and dedicated army set out in high spirits. The audience said farewell to Lynn in her final performance in *Romeo and Juliet* at Covent Garden with a great roar in which affection and regret equally mingled, her devoted admirers massed in the upper reaches of the house. She was not to dance again in London for three years.

MacMillan headed the advance guard, finding the company there were not in such bad shape as had been reported. There were ten principals, eight soloists and a *corps de ballet* of forty-one. The girls were rather more talented than the boys, which is usual in ballet companies, and they had their own South American ballerina, Didi Carli. The theatre was well-equipped, although somewhat cold and impersonal. There was a real sense of a new beginning, since MacMillan's reputation was well-established in Germany, and the dancers worked with great enthusiasm under his assistant, Ray Barra. MacMillan would like to have regenerated the company, as Cranko had done when he took over at Stuttgart, with an intake of foreign dancers, but here he met opposition and did not press the matter further.

To celebrate the occasion Lynn bought a fur coat, redeeming her life insurance policy to pay for it. The possession of it filled her with guilt and joy in about equal measure, which is how she likes things. When she got to Berlin on 7th August, she found Kenneth MacMillan had rented a vast, ten-room flat for himself, Lynn and Ray Barra. It was situated on the Reichsstrasse, only two stops on the underground from the opera house. She was well prepared; she had spent ten days at a health farm to slim down and had also begun German lessons.

At first Kenneth MacMillan took over the existing repertoire, consisting of *Giselle*, Cranko's *Firebird*, *L'Estro Armonico* and *The Lady and the Fool*, together with Lifar's *Suite en Blanc*. Lynn was very well received in two performances of *Giselle*. She was delighted with her new partners, Falco Kapuste, whom she described (displaying her tendency to exaggerate) as 'Nijinsky reincarnate, like a faun, long neck and back and almost thick legs, huge elevation and an electric sense of movement', and Rudolf Holtz, who 'brought reality to all Kenneth's imaginations and dreams'. The first great night for the new regime was on 30th November 1966, when in addition to *The Invitation* two new ballets by MacMillan received their premières. These were *Concerto*, to Shostakovich's second piano concerto, a charming piece with a sweetly romantic middle movement that the composer had written for his son, and *Valses Nobles et Sentimentales*, to the over-familiar score by Ravel, much used by previous choreographers including Balanchine and Ashton.

MacMillan had originally created the whole of this ballet to Ravel's suite *Ma Mère L'Oye* but within a few days of the first performance he was informed that the publishers had refused to grant copyright permission. Lynn says 'it was a living horror' for him, since he had either to create different choreography to new music or transform the existing choreography to fit another score. With amazing ingenuity and technical skill he chose the latter course. He cut, compressed, and extended his basic choreography, so that in a few days it was at one with the music. It is an astounding feat of concentration, craftsmanship and courage; as Lynn remarks, most other choreographers would have taken to the hills faced with such a challenge.

Lynn, slimmer, more elegant than ever and in marvellous

148

technical form, stunned the German critics in *The Invitation*, where the other expatriate, Vergie Derman, gave a beautiful performance as the wife, providing a kind of serene English-type beauty in the midst of a production rather harsher in tone than before. MacMillan had made certain changes, eliminating much of the 'acrobat' sequences that had never worked very well, while Georgiadis sharpened his décor. The effect was stunning.

MacMillan has been inspired to create his wonderful duet for the middle section of *Concerto* by watching Lynn one day in the studio when she was working alone and thinking herself unobserved, and the serene unfolding of her limbs obviously influenced the whole tone of this exquisite *pas de deux*. The dance grows almost organically out of the music, like a flower from the earth, proliferating in images of haunting beauty. This idea of slow dawning is echoed by the lighting design, in which a patch of light slowly spreads across the backcloth like the rising sun. It is one of the most beautiful of all MacMillan's compositions—the celebration of the dance in terms of rebirth, the invocation of one great dancer in the solitude of her art.

He uses with great beauty the mirror effect of three couples in canon as a background for the main *pas de deux*. The other two sections of the work are less inventive, although the first movement has a charming, insouciant ending when all the dancers march off stage like circus ponies leaving the arena, heads held high, with the music tossing like plumes above them. There was no doubting the success of the evening nor the joyous acceptance by the Berlin public of their new ballerina.

Lynn loved Berlin; her new coat sustained her marvellously through the freezing winter. Her German was improving, so that she was even beginning to write out shopping lists for Frau Schneider, their maid, who later made any corrections needed without informing her. She and Vergie Derman found the Germans a bit stuffy and formal. When they wore mini-skirts on a night at the opera, they shocked some members of the more formally dressed audience. Both of them were very fashion conscious and had felt their dresses were too long, so they had chopped off a few inches before the next unveiling. Lynn's dark beauty and her marvellous seeking eyes, and Vergie's grace, fair hair and beautiful features made them much loved by their new public, who recognised how their contrasting styles established a rich harmony in the company's dancing. Lynn had grown very fond of Vergie Derman, whom she had not known particularly well before they went to Germany; her gentleness, sense of fun and serene beauty did much to lighten those first difficult months. All the same it was one of the happiest and most creative periods of her life. Lynn was exhausted most of the time—for her a most satisfactory experience.

But then, with the same ugly precision, disaster struck again. No sooner was the triumphant first night over than Lynn developed a severe infection that was finally diagnosed as glandular fever, the most debilitating and dangerous illness for anyone in her profession. It leads to total physical exhaustion and weakness, and convalescence may take many months. Lynn returned to England for treatment. Her parents were very worried, not only because of the serious nature of the illness itself, but because they felt responsible for the griefs Lynn had experienced over the last few years, fearing they had allowed her to leave home too young so that she had had insufficient attention, both physical and emotional, at such a crucial time in her life. Of this she was able to reassure them completely, stressing that had she not been forced to deal with her difficulties when young, it is unlikely that she would have been able to cope with misfortune with such resilience in later years. She makes the interesting remark that perhaps her agonising homesickness and misery in those first months was, in fact, self-inflicted in order to subdue her own guilt at abandoning her parents.

The solitary nature of the artist's inner life is very real to her. She says:

> I get more peace from the aloneness of dancing and the theatre and certainly far more security depending on myself than on someone I'll never really know. It's not a perfect life—nor is it always alone—but what life is perfect.

Her problem had been faced by many artists in the theatre before her. As she writes:

> My main problem is finding a way to be a ballerina and a woman, because I'm just not the type to live a

150

one-sided life. But I think men who are prepared to accept all that a ballerina *must* give to her work (and it would be like a gift to him, the result of her work and success are the gift) must be very rare indeed.

Her friends rallied round including, of course, Miss Edwards, Christopher Gable (who had now left the Royal Ballet to make a new career on the stage) and Georgina Parkinson, an old friend in the Royal Ballet who looked after her devotedly. By mid-February she was able to do very light exercises, but after nearly six weeks in bed her muscles barely responded; sometimes she felt that she would never regain her strength. By the end of the month she was back in Berlin after a series of gentle classes with Winifred Edwards. When she joined the company classes she did the simplest exercises but was never in the early stages able to let grip of the *barre*. At the end of a week of this her arms seemed stronger than her legs. Apart from twenty minutes alone in the studio, still clinging to the *barre*, she did no further work during the day, as even this exhausted her. For the remainder of the time she read and slept; as she puts it, 'I just lie flat and feel worried.'

Kenneth MacMillan, already under great pressure as director of the company, was deeply upset by her illness, not only for her but also because he had lost his muse. It even seemed to her that he resented her illness, took it as a personal affront; it was as if she had deserted him, using ill health as an excuse for flight. These misunderstandings caused tension between them, so that when she returned to Berlin after her long absence their friendship was under strain; but a relationship as long and close as theirs survives such misunderstandings and unconscious resentments, particularly when they come at a time when both are harassed by other worries. Lynn speaks of these troubled years in Berlin in her direct and honest way, '... he despaired of me an awful lot. I can't say I blame him. I don't blame anyone.'

The first performance of *Anastasia*, to music by Martinu, was given at the Opera House on 25th June 1967. The ballet was modernistic in concept, using projections, newsreels, musical and vocal collage, and spare, functional designs by Barry Kay. It was possibly influenced by the story that had recently appeared in the newspapers in which a woman claimed through law her entitlement as Anastasia, youngest daughter of the Tsar Nicholas and only survivor of the night when the entire family was shot. The ballet is shown in fantasy through the muddled dreams of Anastasia; whether what she dreams in flashback is imagination or reality matters little. Lynn Seymour, partnered by Rudolf Holtz, brought to the part her great dramatic gifts. With her new cropped hair and dressed in an ugly blue dress, she moved from insanity to terrible sad wisdom and back again with that total commitment to a role she had first shown in *The Invitation*.

As the company had no money to fund new productions, all the costumes were rented from a television firm that had done a play set in the same period. The scenery was the back of that from the opera's production of *La Traviata* and the iron gates at the rear of the stage were opened to create an effect of great depth. The revolve was used, so that the bed on which the demented heroine lies (in the later Covent Garden revival driven by a small motor) swivelled round, in Lynn's words, 'like a leaf on a string', while all the protagonists in the ballet walked on the revolve to give an extraordinary nightmare effect.

Her health problems were not over; now she had developed a swelling of the arm that was finally diagnosed as thrombosis. She laughed the matter off by saying: 'I am dancing with one little and one big arm.' This had begun to affect her during the rehearsals for *Anastasia*, just when she had recovered from glandular fever, so that she was obliged once again to return to see a specialist in London. A distant and seemingly far-fetched diversion from all these problems was an invitation from the dancer and choreographer, Herbert Ross, and the playwright, Terence Rattigan, to play the central role in a musical drama with a ballet background, first for the stage and then as a film. She was to be offered a contract to include voice training prior to rehearsals, starting in July 1968. The whole idea seemed hugely improbable, like a scene from some old Hollywood film, but she gladly accepted the invitation to discuss it in New York, where she spent a week in August. She was never very keen on the project which eventually foundered, though a film (*The Turning Point*) was made by Herbert Ross on a similar theme many years later.

Lynn then returned for a short holiday in Monte Carlo, where she stayed at Rudolf Nureyev's villa. Here she met a former prisoner of war who had recently taken up dancing after a career as a writer, sculptor and musician. He was Eike Waltz, and he was to have a profound influence on her future.

The swelling in her arm continued to trouble her for the rest of the year and this she felt did not help her 'line' when she danced the role of Aurora on the first night of Kenneth MacMillan's new production of *The Sleeping Beauty* on 8th October. MacMillan rightly kept close to the original Petipa choreography, as presented by the Royal Ballet, but he made several beautiful additions to the final scene, notably a magnificently conceived *pas de sept* of real Kirov elegance. Lynn Seymour was not at her best on the first night; indeed she was later to say (with characteristic exaggeration) that she ruined it.

Eike had joined her in Berlin and was to dance with the company. At this time he was a great support to her, as she had been much upset by her performance in *The Sleeping Beauty*. After a provincial tour of Germany she returned to Berlin for Christmas. They had a wonderfully happy time together. For a change the decorations of a new flat were progressing at a great pace, with shelves and cupboards magically appearing; it was a good time, despite the fact that the trouble in her arm still had not cleared. The relationship promised a new future for them both but as there were still delays in her divorce from Colin Jones, there was then no possibility of marriage. Lynn was irritated beyond measure by these endless legal complications, which cast the one shadow over her happiness.

In February 1968 Kenneth MacMillan revived his ballet *Las Hermanas*; it had been first produced at Stuttgart in 1963 and was based on the play by Garciá Lorca, *La Casa de Bernarda Alba*, with music by Frank Martin. The role of the frustrated, embittered elder sister (somewhat similar to Hagar in Tudor's *Pillar of Fire* that Lynn was to dance a few years later) gave her a chance to turn her dancing inwards in anguished curves, to break in open movements that were like screams of pain. It contains one *pas de deux* for her of intense, almost brutal passion, but in other ways the character, like those of the other four sisters, is thinly developed, so that she had little to work on in the opening sections of the ballet.

The strain of directing the company was obviously affecting MacMillan's creative powers; this was sadly evident in *Olympiad*, presented in Berlin the following month, in which athletic endeavour was not very successfully translated into

movement. Lynn Seymour took part in a danced tennis match, a kind of mixed-doubles for two duets. Although the ballet contained some fine passages, the whole was well below MacMillan's usual standard.

This was to be Lynn's last created new role in Berlin; she was now pregnant. Her twin boys, Adrian and Jerszy, were born on 31st August 1969. They had a quartet of distinguished godparents, Rudolf Nureyev and Kenneth MacMillan, Vergie Derman and Georgina Parkinson, four of Lynn's dearest friends. She was overjoyed, dismissing her mother's worries about the danger to her career posed by the responsibility of two children. But before the twins were installed at home she had one or two anxious moments:

> Everyone from the paediatrician on down, raised their eyes to heaven and clasped their hands together at the word 'twins' and patted me soothingly on the back.

A dance magazine commented dryly that Lynn was not the kind of lady who does things by halves. The company, hugely delighted, rallied round; one of the boys gave her a double baby carriage and Ray Barra bought an enormous playpen. Her great friends, Marcia Haydée and Richard Craigun, came over from Stuttgart, complete with two high chairs and various other attachments. Dame Margot Fonteyn had been over to Berlin for their ballet week and she, Nureyev and Lynn had lunch together; they cooed appropriately over the babies and were amazed at how young and slim she looked. Indeed, she had never felt better, as she discovered when she began working again in November. Even her technique seemed to have improved. She had, it is true, some thoughts of retiring from the ballet, as she hated the long absences from the babies, but she was soon deeply involved again. By January 1969 she was on stage once more. In March she danced in *Giselle*, partnered by Rudolf Nureyev, with the Dutch National Ballet in Amsterdam. Then in May came Kenneth MacMillan's new version of *Swan Lake* for the Oper Ballet. It was a

---

*Lynn, as the elder, embittered, sister, in Kenneth MacMillan's* Las Hermanas, *first created for Marcia Haydée and the Stuttgart Ballet in 1963.*

splendidly original production in which the whole story is presented as Prince Siegfried's dream. Although still a little weak for the virtuosity of the third act, Lynn gave a beautiful poetic performance in her finest melting style. She was partnered by a young dancer, Frank Frey and the great second act duet worked exquisitely. Frey was young, inexperienced as a dancer, but hugely talented; he became a great friend of Lynn's. Much to her taste, he was a bit wild and impetuous— as she puts it, 'a wonderfully crazy person, always in trouble'.

This was to be MacMillan's final gift to the Berlin ballet, for which he had achieved so much since 1966. He left the company prior to taking up his new appointment as joint director of the Royal Ballet in London the following year when Sir Frederick Ashton retired.

There followed a very busy time for Lynn. At the recommendation of Rudolf Nureyev, who was always looking for means to help her, she was invited by Roland Petit to dance to music by Iannis Xenakis in a new ballet, *Kraanerg*, commissioned for the opening of the Canadian National Arts Centre in Ottawa on 2nd June. Ever since his emergence just after the war as the young hope of French Ballet, director of *Les Ballets des Champs Elysées*, surrounded by a group of the most celebrated artists in Paris and guided by Diaghilev's former assistant, Boris Kochno, Petit had stunned both Paris and London with a series of astonishing creations, notably *Les Forains*, *Le Jeune Homme et la Mort*, and later the sensational *Carmen*, *Le Loup* and *Les Demoiselles de la Nuit*, created for Margot Fonteyn. After that he had never quite fulfilled his astonishing potential, but was—and still is—a major force in French ballet.

*Kraanerg* was a new departure for him: a taut, almost distorted work that matched the eerie score of Xenakis, a mixture of orchestral sounds and taped *musique concrète*, savage and disturbing, at times sounding like hugely magnified dentists' drills and with much the same effect to the ear as to the teeth. It is, however, a remarkable work, a powerful futuristic vision, richly structured in eleven sections by a

---

*In Berlin Lynn rehearses* Swan Lake *with her partner, Frank Frey, who joined the Berlin Opera Ballet as a soloist in 1967 at the age of twenty.*

choreographer whose handling of group movements is usually rather dull and conventional. The harsh angularities of the choreography matched a set composed of shifting black and white lines, plus two floating objects, one spheroid and the other rectangular. Lynn enjoyed it hugely, finding it the perfect contrast to the classical ballets of Petipa of which she was becoming increasingly bored. She was partnered by Georges Piletta, while the other main role was danced by one of the finest and most poetic of all the dancers of the Canadian National Ballet, Veronica Tennant.

Lynn's disillusionment with pure classicism was shown in an interview at that time in which she said:

> Ballet, as far as I'm concerned, is the most boring, decadent art form that exists. It's essentially a dead form with a dead hierarchy. The whole hierarchy thing—first dancers, second dancers and so on—is especially bad in Europe. It's one of the reasons why I do not want to stay with one company any more.

These remarks must be seen in the context of her performance in *The Sleeping Beauty* in Berlin that had much upset her, since she felt her first appearance in it had let the company down, and she spread the blame wider than perhaps she would have done at another time. Even several years later she says of her performance, 'I wake up in the night, quaking, thinking of it.' A great dramatic dancer is indeed severely limited by the traditional classical roles, and her desire to extend her range was drawing her more and more to the modern dance. She loved working with Petit; she admired his charm, his endless creativity and his marvellous plastic imagination. With him she was able to learn a very difficult role with great speed. The first night was a very grand occasion, attended by Prime Minister Trudeau.

Then she was back in London to dance with the Festival Ballet, having also fitted in performances with the Oper Ballet at the Vienna Festival when she replaced the injured Mimi Paul in *The Sleeping Beauty*. One of the greatest dancers of

---

*Guest artist with the National Ballet of Canada in Roland Petit's* Kraanerg, *partnered by Georges Piletta to music by Xenakis and striking décor by Vasarely, using mirror and shadow effects, 1969.*

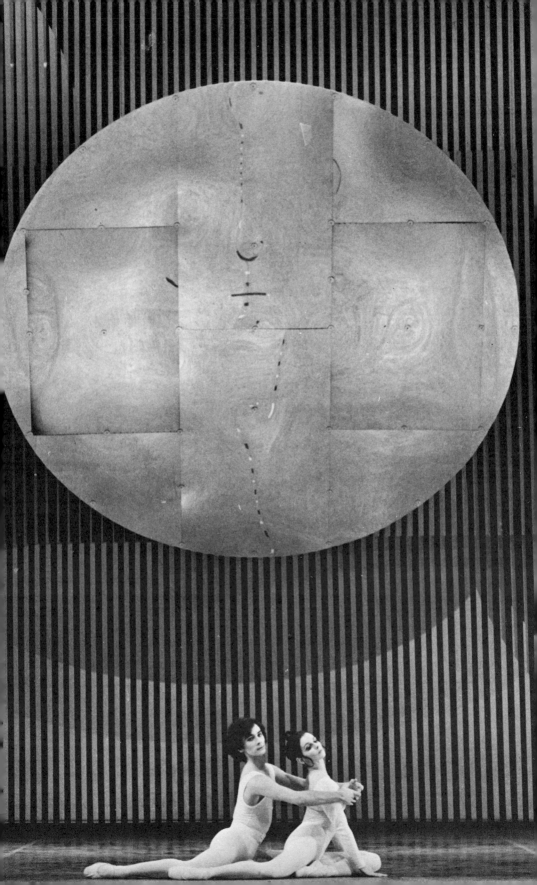

American ballet, loved by London audiences since her first appearance there with the New York City Ballet in 1965, particularly for her magical performance in *Bugaku*, she was a difficult person to replace by anyone of equal stature. There seemed to be only one choice from the available dancers, and Lynn's first appearance in London for three years gained her a tumultuous ovation. Partnered by Peter Martins, she brought the same warmth and youthful ardour to the role that the public had loved in the past, now coupled with a new authority that her experience as *prima ballerina* in Berlin had given her. One question was asked insistently: when was she to appear regularly in London again?

Her future was equally problematic to herself. Upon MacMillan's departure she had been dismissed by the Oper Ballet, while she and Eike had their two children to support. An enormous success with the Oper Ballet during the Vienna Festival in June had, however, forced the Oper Ballet to make a somewhat shame-faced retraction and they re-engaged her as a guest artist.

This career suited her pefectly. She had always loved her independence, and the blood of her pioneering grandfather was in her veins. By now she was tired of being a member of an established ballet company. She expressed her views in an interview with considerable force:

> There may be difficulties, but I'm greedy for performances. I feel I must have them, because I consider the next five or six years will be my best.

Now she was tired: illness, emotional worries, financial problems and grinding hard work seemed a lot to pay for so insecure a career. 'It's no bed of roses,' she told an interviewer. But in temperament she is not unlike another artist who also suffered so terribly from illness and misfortune but who never let her single-minded devotion to her art break her unconquerable spirit. When Katherine Mansfield died so young and with a small collection of immortal stories as her memorial, her favourite quotation from Shakespeare's *Henry IV* was carved above her grave:

> *Out of this nettle, danger, we pluck*
> *this flower, safety.*

She could not retire.

# 6: The Prodigal's Return

*N HER NEW* career as an itinerant guest artist Lynn was finding roles very different from Aurora and Odette. She greatly enjoyed it, despite the anxieties of periods without engagements, the makeshift productions in which she sometimes appeared and the exhausting travel schedules involved.

During the year after leaving the Berlin Oper Ballet she visited Canada no less than seven times. In November 1969 she was in Toronto to dance in *Kraanerg* with the Canadian National Ballet, also appearing in *La Sylphide*, partnered by Hazaros Surmejan. This, Rudolf Nureyev believes, is one of the greatest roles and it is sad that she has never danced the complete ballet before her devoted London public, since it would be likely to stand comparison with the performances of Natalia Makarova and Eva Evdokimova as the finest to be seen at the present time. Her flowing style, the beautiful rounded arms of the Danish school and her fine *élévation* are ideal attributes for one of the most difficult roles in a ballerina's repertoire.

Early in the New Year she returned to dance in Peter Wright's production of *Giselle* with Egon Madsen for the Canadian National Ballet at the O'Keefe Centre in Toronto. As seemed always to happen in Canada she received a bad press, as did Madsen, one of Europe's greatest dancers, but by now Lynn expected it. She has, she feels (and here Nureyev agrees with her), danced many of her greatest performances in Canada; never has she received there the sort of acclaim she has known both in Europe and the United States. Once again she appeared in *La Sylphide*, where critical comment was more favourable but certainly far from ecstatic.

In May she was in Vancouver to appear with the newly formed Western Dance Theatre, a modern dance company founded the previous year by Norbert Vesak, a friend of hers for many years. Vesak found it difficult to introduce Canadian audiences to modern dance. His work had met with scorn and disapproval, so that to have a ballerina of Lynn Seymour's reputation appear with his company gave it the kind of accolade he needed. They danced together in *Poème*, an early work in the modern style, to music by Samuel Barber and completely divorced from the classical technique in which she had been educated, with choreography by Pauline Koner. It was an interesting encounter for both of them, since the choreographer had never created with a classically trained dancer before. Three performances were given at the Queen Elizabeth Theatre on 24th, 25th, and 26th May and Lynn assimilated the new style with assured ease. She was also partnered by Vesak in a *pas de deux* from *Solitaire*. On this trip Lynn brought the twins with her to meet their grandparents for the first time.

While in Canada she met Felix Blaska, a former assistant to Roland Petit, who was there to mount a production of Petit's *Le Loup*, and he invited her to dance with his small company in Paris, where he would create a ballet for her. She accepted eagerly, since Blaska is a gifted choreographer who has been greatly influenced by Petit, but who has extended his ideas further and in a most original manner. It was, again, a challenge—a different style, a new aspect of the dance.

Lynn appeared with his group in March 1970 at the Théâtre de la Ville in Paris. These ballet evenings took place from six to seven pm, being known rather nicely as 'cocktail matinées'. She took over the leading role in his *Ballet for Tam-Tam and Percussion*, when the dancer scheduled to appear in this was injured just before the first performance. The choreographer attempted to mix the sounds of African tam-tams and electrified percussion instruments, to which a series of classical variations were constructed for her and Georges Piletta, her partner for *Kraanerg* the previous year. Blaska himself danced with a small chorus of five men and two girls. Less adventurous was a grand *pas d'action* to music by Schumann; it was considered rather more paste than jewellery and did not win much support from either the critics or the public. At this time, however, she was not in her best form, and this

162

embarrassed her as the other dancers in the Company seemed disappointed with their guest artist from whom they had expected so much.

One of the great delights of this visit to Paris was the opportunity it gave her to study again under Raymond Franchetti, a teacher who has always been an inspiration to her. Director of dance at the Paris Opéra from 1971 until 1976, he has maintained the famous traditions of the French School and enriched them by his profound insight into the nature of classicism. His own school in Paris brought visiting dancers from many companies to study with him (not only celebrated ballerinas but also great male artists like Mikhail Baryshnikov) and he has also been a much admired guest teacher at the Royal Ballet School. He and Stanley Williams, a teacher formerly with the Royal Danish Ballet and later with the New York City Ballet, have been a continual inspiration to her.

In July Lynn danced as a guest artist with the Festival Ballet at the Coliseum but she appeared only in a *pas de deux* from *La Sylphide*, partnered by Peter Breuer, and the absurd duet, the *Walpurgisnacht* from Gounod's *Faust*, one of the most dated, cliché-benumbed concert pieces in the repertoire of the Bolshoi Ballet. It looked more like a sequence from a Buster Keaton film or the finale of an end-of-the-pier review of generations ago, where the chorus girls in blonde wigs might be pursued into the wings by puffing dancers of indeterminate age and sex. It was hilarious and Lynn Seymour danced it for all it wasn't worth. One recalled the bewitching Yekaterina Maximova, a truly glorious classical ballerina, romping through the Bolshoi Ballet production of *Don Quixote*, thrusting the absurd choreography aside with impudent daring; it was not just mock-Spanish, but mockery itself, the insouciance of great art trifling with the commonplace. The supreme classicist of our age, Natalia Makarova, treats its famous *pas de deux* in the same way; nothing is more delightful than her bemused expression—a kind of wildness in her eyes after some amazing technical feat—that calls out in desperation to the audience, 'Tell me, what am I supposed to do next?' Lynn Seymour had equal fun with *Walpurgisnacht*, hamming it up to sensational effect, her gravity at any moment liable to collapse into laughter. Technically the dancing was a miracle of flowing lines and airy poise, for you cannot mock anything until you can do it superlatively well.

By that time she had decided after some hesitation to return to the Royal Ballet. She had loved her freelance career; it had brought her unusual roles, many friends and widened her horizons in terms of dance styles that were to be of great value to her in the future. But she missed being away from the twins and having no settled home. Now that Kenneth MacMillan had taken over as director at the Royal Ballet at Covent Garden, she felt it might offer her wider scope than in her last year there before Berlin. She was avid for performances, anxious to experiment; more important still was the need to work with choreographers of the highest standard, not always possible for a guest artist who has to accept work from wherever it comes, and she hoped that her collaboration with Kenneth MacMillan could be resumed in a more creative atmosphere than that in Berlin. It was a new beginning at the Royal Ballet; she has never been one to miss such a challenge.

This was not part of some master plan of her own, since the invitation to return was not expected. Indeed, her career has been a series of brilliant improvisations, sudden breaks of fortune, moments of impulse that have sustained it and enriched her creativity as an artist. She was so often planning in great detail one future, only to live quite another; what remained constant was her dedication (she hates the word, since she thinks it has a 'nunnish' flavour) to the dance. In an interview with John Gale for the *Observer* she affirmed her attitude to dancing with great clarity; he was to use what she said, almost word for word, in his posthumous novel *Camera Man*, when his heroine, Belinda, says:

> To me, people's idea of ballet is terribly out of date. I think that ballet, when it's at its best, is the most total theatre you can have. The body can say something a million times more expressively than words. With the body you can express love, sensuality, sexuality, or whatever, as well as things that are minute but important—things that you can miss with words. You can never mistake what the body does. I'll go into any ugly shape that's wanted; I'll fall over or become twisted. I'll do that so that the choreographer can find out what *he* wants. I also want to be able to help him and inspire him and be part of it. The dancer is the instrument, but this

instrument must add; I don't want the choreographer to take this thing and make it exactly what *he* wants it to be, because it's flesh and blood, wheezing and palpitating, and nasty. It must be expected to add or inspire, and can't just be there as a lump with legs sticking out. Yet I'm a person who likes to be used. I'm not an instigator.

This total commitment to a role was never more apparent than when she returned to *Romeo and Juliet* at Covent Garden on 12th October 1970, partnered by David Wall. In that eerie duet in the last act when her partner dances with her seemingly dead body, she was reduced to a limp mass of flesh, lying on the ground, grotesque and inhuman. As Christopher Gable remembers, of all the ballerinas who have danced this part she is the only one who does not care at all how ugly, even how misshapen she looks in her corpse-like trance; there is not a hint of the ballerina seeking for a classical line: realism, however grotesque, even shameful, it might look in terms of the image of the classical ballerina, is all that counts with her. At the close of the ballet the audience welcomed her back with such joy she might have been absent for twenty years.

A week later on 19th October she danced in the first performance of Jerome Robbins' masterpiece, *Dances at a Gathering*, to a selection of piano music by Chopin. This exquisite work is one of the most tender glances at youth and the passing of youth ever to be enacted on the modern stage. Lynn Seymour took her place as one of a group of dancers, each of whom makes their own contribution to this series of fleeting encounters, games and flirtations that end in the terrible presentiment of death, the darkness that for one still and haunted moment they watch cross the sky and realise that the long day of their playing is over. They are at the end adults; quietly they leave the stage in pairs, each to their unknown future. All life is here in one hour on the stage— meeting, loving, parting; above all, the quiet and final acceptance that:

> *Golden lads and girls all must*
> *As chimney-sweepers, come to dust.*

By turns she was merry, childlike, wilful, boisterous and suddenly lonely—the one left out, something that is so much a part of her character and of the roles, such as the girl in *Solitaire*, she has made her own. In the Opus 70 waltz she found more humour than even the choreographer had imagined within it. Ignored by her three male partners in turn, she is so full of herself yet so eager to catch their attention; obviously she bores them stiff. They wander off, leaving her as it were in mid sentence, enthralling the empty air with an anecdote of excruciating banality. Ignored by her men, she flaunts off the stage. It doesn't matter, she implies; it's their loss not mine as I'm obviously so interesting.

This section of the ballet was inspired by the great French ballerina, Violette Verdy, whose enchanting and effervescent personality spills out in a torrent of talk to everyone within range. It is delightful but a little wearing for more silent or less extroverted personalities, who have been immortalised by Robbins in the three male dancers who withdraw with a polite and vacant smile, leaving her unattended on the floodtide of anecdote.

When they learned the ballet from Robbins, none of the dancers was sure what parts they were finally to dance. Lynn rehearsed the dances later to be taken by Monica Mason but at the last moment Robbins changed his mind, brushing aside her objections. This did not worry her; she takes autocratic choreographers to her heart as willingly as any others, provided of course that they show the necessary talent.

Over Christmas and the New Year she returned to *The Invitation* and *The Two Pigeons*, once again setting the clock back with that gift for enclosing a world in a single gesture. As far as the audience was concerned everything was as before; they were enchanted with her.

Then a new, rare experience offered itself. Lynn had always admired Alvin Ailey and his company of dancers and she was delighted by an invitation to dance the lead in a new ballet *Flowers*, where the central role was to be created for her. This she performed in New York early in 1971. The immediate inspiration of the ballet was the tragic life of Janis Joplin, who was destroyed by drink, drugs and all the temptations that accompany fame in the world of pop entertainment. It is set to the rock music of Big Brother and the Holding Company, Pink Floyd, Blind Faith and Janis Joplin herself, and dedicated to the big stars of that world: Jimi Hendrix, Bob Dylan and Mick Jagger. Lynn revelled in it, although she had trouble learning

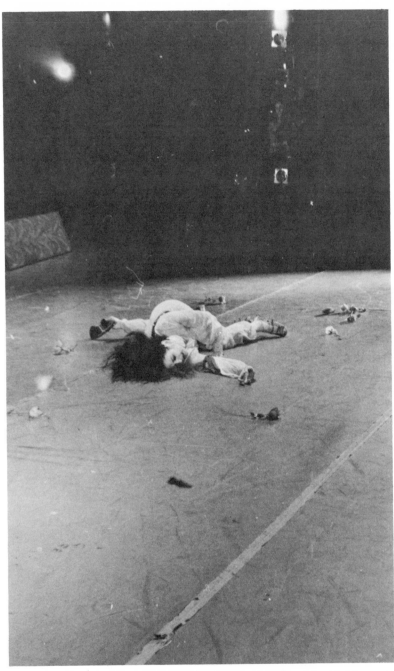

*In Alvin Ailey's modern dance work,* Flowers, *performed with his Company and based on the tragic life of Janis Joplin, 1971.*

the role, particularly as she was dancing in high-heeled shoes; the inward nature of modern dance, with its emphasis on stress and oppositions in movement, was particularly difficult to her as she was brought up in an entirely different tradition. Ailey kept urging her to stop tiptoeing around, stop being dainty and work from her hips. She loves his company, the individuality of his dancers and his huge creative zest. Her performance in the role at the Sadler's Wells Theatre in London two years later is described in *Camera Man*:

> The music, canned, was the voice—and backing—of some desperate singer, dead of drink, drugs, and, no doubt, love: Belinda danced the singer. . . . Her partner was a lean and tremendous black in steel-rimmed dark glasses who hurled her about magnificently. ... Belinda, the singer, was brave and desperate: brave and desperate, as Belinda so often liked to be, herself, on and off the stage. As Belinda danced, you believed in her, in her 'warmth and quality.' . . . She fell, drank, snorted coke, kicked over chairs and tables, writhed, shrank from endless black photographers and endless flash bulbs, who wore large hats and enveloping coats, and, in the end, she died. . . . She was a terrific actress: she had done it, with passion and conviction, whatever she may have thought of the part. She still had the soft quality that he remembered. But she was, also, frightening. . . . Her body and being were to him that night so powerful and intolerant; the face so restless and demanding. What did that face want?

While she was in *Flowers* in New York, she was also commuting to Toronto to dance in *Giselle* with the Canadian National Ballet, partnered by Peter Martins, and back to London again for performances at Covent Garden. A typical schedule was a Thursday night's performance in *Flowers* in New York, an arrival at 10.30 am next morning in Toronto for rehearsals in *Giselle* danced that evening, a return to New York the next day for a matinée and evening performance, back in Toronto the next morning for a matinée in *Giselle*. On the same night she flew to London for the following day's *Raymonda* at Covent Garden. And, while this hectic schedule was in progress, Kenneth MacMillan was creating his full-length *Anastasia* for her, so that sometimes he despaired a little to see his muse disappear for these dancing weekends half way across the world. He wondered at which airport she would be stranded, while his new ballet hung immobilised before him. However, she always made it, as she always makes class, in time—just.

MacMillan's *Anastasia* was first performed at Covent Garden on 22nd July 1971. MacMillan had extended the original one-act ballet, first produced in Berlin, by adding two opening acts to Tchaikovsky's 1st and 3rd symphonies. The result was not a success, certainly not with the public—where the upper reaches of the house booed the choreographer at his curtain call—nor in the opinion of the majority of the critics. It did not make a coherent whole; the first two thirds of the ballet were so different in mood, style and music to the expressionistic last. There were, however, no doubts at all of Lynn Seymour's own performance as Anna Anderson. From her first entry on roller-skates and wearing a sailor suit to the last demented scenes, she gave a dominating performance, even though the ballet is not well-constructed round the central role.

After *Anastasia* a depressing lull set in both for Lynn and the company. Everyone had been upset by the ballet's poor reception, while MacMillan was under constant criticism, both from outside and within the organisation. He had not, he recalls, made many friends among the dancers by creating his first major ballet for Lynn in preference to those who had carried the repertoire during her absence in Berlin. But Lynn was not aware of any jealousy. As she says dryly: 'If there is a fire, I'm always the last one who smells the smoke.' It was, however, a troublesome time for MacMillan and the problem of trying to create new ballets and run the Company against a background of criticism in the press put him under continual strain. Even though Lynn had returned to many of her great roles—*Swan Lake* with Rudolf Nureyev, *Giselle* with David Wall, as well as Balanchine's beautiful *Serenade*, where her flowing style caught the lines of Tchaikovsky's music as if it were its shadow imprinted on the air—the new works were only oddments, such as MacMillan's *Side Show* for herself and Nureyev, memorable only for his curly moustache. She was still offered guest engagements abroad (even though a permanent member of the Company), notably with the

Belgrade Ballet in March 1972, where she and David Blair had a great success in *Giselle* and *Swan Lake*.

To make matters worse, the Company's usual spring and early summer tour of North America in 1972 was not an enormous success, partly through bad programme planning but also through an unreasoned hostility of the public to the Royal Ballet's new director who, for all his remarkable gifts as a choreographer, lacked the warm and endearing public image of his beloved predecessors. He was not good at dealing with people, being shy, introverted and withdrawn, so that only his close friends, such as Lynn, were aware of his warm and generous heart. A section of the ballet public developed a vast antagonism to him; what enraged them most was that he was not present on the opening night. This they considered an act of extreme discourtesy, comparing such behaviour with that of his predecessors, who felt a New York opening took priority over any other engagement, however important. The ballet, Anastasia, angered them, too—not that they were in any mood to judge it objectively.

His ballets, as already noted, provoke and disturb by their insistence upon a painful reality in human behaviour. They do not entertain in the expected sense and the Royal Ballet with its lavish productions of the classics was in American eyes the company *par excellence* to offer grand escapism in its repertoire. Further, the New York public has for many years been educated by Balanchine to demand pure classical dancing, unencumbered by any dark imaginings or even drama; the ideals of the dance-drama as set out by Fokine were long ago rejected and MacMillan's insistence upon them met with ugly opposition. Balletomania (as Lynn was herself to discover in Munich some years later) is not a rational enthusiasm; it is fanaticism, not unlike that of the football fan or the devout at a revivalist meeting. Nothing much has changed in this respect since the audience fought with one another during the first performance of *Le Sacre du Printemps* in 1913. This predictable hysteria, common to the lunatic fringe of all ballet audiences and endowed, in Dame Ninette's phrase, 'with more lungs than logic', was intensified by the special feeling the New York public has for the Royal Ballet. They love the Company, their most frequent guest from abroad, in a deeply possessive way, like a favourite daughter; any changes in style or direction are bitterly resented. They do not want the Royal Ballet to grow

*A solo from the first act of* Anastasia, *when Kenneth MacMillan lengthened his original work for the Royal Ballet in 1971.*

up but always to remain the endearing adolescent whom they first met on that legendary night in 1949.

As a result of the hostility, morale among the dancers was low. It was a cruel, uneasy time for them all, none more so than Lynn, whose own emotional difficulties were intensified by the edgy atmosphere around her. Inevitably she began to put on weight again; and when she and the other dispirited dancers returned to London, she decided to end her relationship with Eike Waltz and they agreed to part. The conflicting demands of her personality, her self-sufficiency on the one hand and her quest for security on the other, were the cause of the rupture. Yet she did not become embittered. She had learned the same truth as Katherine Mansfield who wrote in her *Journals*: 'Suffering is a gift which has taught me to look on the world with love.'

Heartbreak lay beneath the merry façade she presented to the world, and she turned to the dance for consolation. A new role in *Laborintus*, a ballet by Glen Tetley, given its first performance at Covent Garden on 26th July 1972, was her huge reward. She loved working with Tetley, a friend of hers for many years and one of the most original and profound choreographers of our time, whose inner symbolic vision reaches such depths of understanding. It is a dark, tormented world he discovered in *Laborintus* that is reminiscent of the terrible nightmares of Hieronymus Bosch as well as the visionary insights of William Blake. In Lynn Seymour's richness and flow of movement he found new inspiration. Partnered by Rudolf Nureyev, she achieved with him a tormented beauty that was like the fusion of two lost souls, clutching for each other in a loveless darkness. They were together, and they were alone, lost in a mirrored void that reflected only its own emptiness. It was a great ballet, marvellously performed by them both.

There were again long gaps between performances. She was troubled by her weight, lost for inspiration. Most cruel of all, certain sections of the press began to make snide remarks about her. She was appearing only in *Dances at a Gathering* and *Song of the Earth*. In the Robbins' ballet she had begun to spoil her wonderful first insight into the role by excessive over-playing that gave the impression that she mocked herself.

At this difficult period Rudolf Nureyev was a tower of strength, fighting her battles, endeavouring to obtain guest appearances abroad for her to which the Company might agree. But it all came to nothing. It seemed that her career was in an inevitable decline: for over a year her only new created role was that of a cabaret performer in MacMillan's indifferent version of *The Seven Deadly Sins*, first given at Covent Garden in July 1973. It was a tiny part, providing her only with the opportunity to wave tassels from her breasts and waggle her hips. Richard Buckle observed drily: 'She wags a cute back-side.'

Her life outside the ballet began to absorb her more and more. During the year she had met a successful and talented commercial photographer, Philip Pace, with whom she fell in love. Now the ballet that seemed to have deserted her was eclipsed by a new happiness. Perhaps, she thought, after the New Year she should retire.

The offer of a new role in a ballet by Ronald Hynd about the Brontë's to be performed at Sadler's Wells was not enough to attract her. There was, she felt sure, no future for her as a dancer. She and Phillip decided to get married. At last, ironically, she had achieved what before she thought was impossible: she was not dancing and she was happy.

Her third child, Demian, was born in July 1974. Her career, she decided, was over. One recalls what she had said to her friend, Fay Angus, several years earlier when she played with Fay's small son: 'Fay, you live in the real world, out here. This is what it is all about.' She had paused and smiled. 'I adore strong, quiet little boys,' she said. Now she had three of her own. The ballet was not everything: there was a world elsewhere.

# 7: The Second Spring

*A* FEW WEEKS BEFORE Demian was born Lynn had a telephone call from Kenneth MacMillan. Would she, he asked, return to the Royal Ballet when she was in training again? He planned to open the season with the ill-fated *Anastasia*, with some adjustments to the production and choreography. He believed in the work, as she did, but his confidence had been badly shattered by its poor reception. She could help him, he could help her; they needed one another. They could begin again together. It was an invitation from a friend she loved and with whom she had enjoyed the finest creative relationship of her career, during which she had been his central inspiration. She did not hesitate for long. The dreams of retirement from dancing faded. It was a challenge, perhaps the greatest of her whole career, and that was irresistible.

Impulsively, she accepted. And this time, she said to herself, she would be marvellous, greater than ever before. It would involve months of gruelling work, abominable diets and exercises and, above all, a fierce will to succeed. Half a century previously the incomparable ballerina of the Imperial Theatre, Vera Trefilova, had faced the same challenge and she had returned to the stage after a period of retirement a greater ballerina.

Lynn would do the same; she was set on it, absolutely determined. Her friends and colleagues marvelled at her courage, but they were afraid.

---

*The last act of* Anastasia *when Anna Anderson in a Berlin hospital seeks to recall what real or imagined life she had as Anastasia, youngest daughter of the last Tsar of Russia.*

On her return to Covent Garden on 17 January 1975 not only was she slimmer, more elegant, but dancing more brilliantly than she had ever done. She had reached the peak of her artistry, not only in terms of interpretation but of a new command. She danced like a young artist who had just attained the heights, not like a mature dancer who had fought so many battles with her physique, who had been seen to struggle with it often so painfully.

She had worked, as she promised herself she would, with fierce determination. Many teachers helped and she owed in particular a great debt to Terry Westmoreland of the Royal Ballet, who had been her inspiration during those long hard months when sometimes she began to doubt that she would ever be able to return. Classes with him not only strengthened her technique to an extent that surprised even herself but also gave her new insights into movement.

The critics joined the public in their acclaim. James Monahan, now the director of the Royal Ballet School, said:

> ... now she has become an exception to all the rules, for she must be the only ballerina ever to come to her best at the age of 36—and having had three children ... we have a different Seymour now; she has lost none of her special qualities and has acquired slimness (without boniness), lightness, litheness and a lovely capacity for linear 'extension'; her expressiveness has shed its chains. It is all a kind of miracle.

In March Lynn was seen in another aspect of her chameleon-like personality—the delicious, swoony girl, drooling over Chopin (and the pianist) at the first performance of Jerome Robbins' *The Concert* at Covent Garden on 4th March. Later in the ballet, to see her try on a large, ornamental hat like a miniature flower garden was a little surrealistic dance in itself; she was at once zany, skittish and slightly unsure of herself. One might well object to glorious music used as an excuse for knock-about farce but Lynn Seymour remains imperishably in the memory, drooping like a wilted lily across the piano lid.

In June she appeared in the Royal Ballet's 'Big Top' in Battersea Park, dancing a great variety of roles including *Concerto*, *Les Sylphides*, *The Prodigal Son*, *Side Show*, *The Concert* and

176

*Lynn buys her splendid new hat from Derek Rencher during Jerome Robbins' zany ballet* The Concert, *to music by Chopin, first performed by the New York City Ballet in 1956, and revived by the Royal Ballet in 1975.*

Jack Carter's fine dance-drama, *Shukumei*. It was the first time she had danced in this ballet and also in *The Prodigal Son*, where the role of the Siren, although by now sadly dated, gave her the chance to smoulder with an erotic malevolence much to her taste. The murderous Samurai in Jack Carter's ballet, first created by Marion Tait for the touring company, was not exactly a cosy lady either and Lynn Seymour gave her icy revenge a fierce and cutting edge, her feet stabbing the stage like knives.

In addition she took part in a choreographic workshop with Wayne Eagling of the Royal Ballet in which they made new experiments in movement that were to be of value to her when she came to create her own ballets. As if this were not enough, she dashed across by taxi to The Place at Euston

without even time to change out of her costume for *Concerto*, where she appeared in a London Contemporary Dance Theatre gala performance in a duet by Bernd Berg, a friend of hers from her guest appearances with the Stuttgart Ballet.

On 22nd June Lynn took part in a gala performance in Hamburg to celebrate the life of Vaslav Nijinsky. She danced the young girl in *Le Spectre de la Rose* with Mikhail Baryshnikov; his ardent youth and her beauty in this new awakening made a glorious partnership. Dame Margot Fonteyn sent Lynn her own costume for the ballet together with a long letter about the role, containing performance details that Fonteyn had been given by Tamara Karsavina, the creator of the part, when she first danced it with Nijinsky, and who had later taught it to Fonteyn.

But the greatest event of the evening was the new dance in the style of Isadora Duncan that Ashton composed for Lynn. Ashton has always cherished his memories of Duncan and he set one of these recollections to a Brahms' waltz from Opus 39 with Christoph Eschenbach to play it. This solo belongs to Lynn Seymour in the same way as *Mort du Cygne* belongs to Anna Pavlova; one could think of no other ballerina who could perform it with the same warmth, the same rounded flow of movement and soft but distant sensuality. Ashton was to add further dances to the series in 1976 and the solo, *Five Brahms Waltzes in the Style of Isadora Duncan*, now belongs to history. With their air of faded elegance, they are of their period; but in their vitality, richness of open and flowing lines and sensuality, they are among Ashton's finest achievements and certainly Lynn Seymour's glory. In miniature they encapsulate her emotional life in all its richness and complexity beneath the shadow of a long-dead genius, so similar to her in temperament. They are both a memorial and a living work of art, where the strange impassioned ghost of one dancer seems to take over the mind and body of another. Her diaphanous costume was an exact replica of that worn by Duncan, causing her dresser to recoil in shocked disapproval. 'But, madam,' she said, 'You wear no bra.' Isadora Duncan would have approved.

---

*A knockabout duet,* Side Show, *by Kenneth MacMillan, in which Rudolf Nureyev sports an unexpected moustache. First created in 1972.*

From Hamburg Lynn travelled direct to Athens where she joined the Touring Company of the Royal Ballet for their season there, dancing in *Concerto*, *Giselle*, *The Prodigal Son* and the *pas de deux* from *Don Quixote*. These rapid contrasts, both in roles and in the type of engagement she accepted at this period, are emphasised by her part in a Ballet Seminar at Ilkley in Yorkshire, organised by a former Royal Ballet dancer David Gayle, who was born in Ilkley. The Seminar was opened by Dame Ninette de Valois. Dame Alicia Markova, Peter Clegg, Wayne Sleep and Lynn all gave classes and demonstrations to the students.

The greatest test was to come—her return to her most famous role of Juliet. She danced this at Covent Garden on 24th July, when her triumph was complete and excelled even her first appearance in the role a decade previously. She looked if anything younger than she did then; and even though one expected the dramatic qualities of her dancing to be unchanged, the ease with which she floated through the difficult choreography was something quite new.

After a short summer holiday she joined the Royal Ballet at the Edinburgh Festival, where she danced in *Raymonda* and *Giselle* with Rudolf Nureyev; it was a wonderful occasion for her as she found her technique matched the demands of classical ballet with an ease she had not known before. Working with Nureyev had given her new insight into classicism; now she felt she understood it for the first time:

> He has taught me what Petipa's classicism is and what it means, which I had never understood before, as a technical rather than as a theatrical experience in which one must confront the difficulties with complete honesty.

Nureyev showed her the meaning of the total simplicity in classical dancing that was part of his inheritance from the Kirov, but is only to be gained after many years of fining down all inessentials and decorations to the dance. His continual demand to her was 'simplify: don't compromise'. Under his tuition the classics took on a new meaning.

This grand progression was interrupted by illness. From September, after a season at Nottingham, until the end of the year, she was off the stage but when she returned to Covent Garden in the new year in *The Two Pigeons* it was to excel her

*As the mother in the third and final section of Kenneth MacMillan's ballet* Rituals *(1975), to music by Bartok, based on the Japanese ritual theatre.*

younger self whom she now seemed to challenge, recklessly but with an absolute self-confidence, at every performance.

Her last created role of the year was in MacMillan's new ballet, which was obviously inspired by the Company's visit to Japan earlier. *Rituals* was not, however, a great success; his attempt to reconstruct the movements of the Japanese ritual Kabuki theatre and martial arts was oddly superficial. The middle section, based on the ideas of the Japanese Bunraku puppet theatre, provided little more than one dancer-puppet

181

Partnered by David Wall in Manon, *based on the novel by Prévost, first created by Antoinette Sibley in 1974, subsequently danced by Natalia Makarova, Lynn Seymour and Jennifer Penney.*

being carried around like a badly wrapped parcel, although it did have an eerie conclusion. Lynn appeared in the final section, 'Celebration and Prayer', as the mother, with Monica Mason as the midwife; but again the ideas seemed to have been sketched in outline rather than fully developed.

New Year's day 1976 saw her dance the lead in Kenneth MacMillan's *Manon* for the first time. The ballet, first performed in 1974, seems to have been composed by the choreographer full of memories of his absent muse for whom he appears to search in the great, arched and passionate *pas de deux* that speak of her in each curving line, as in the sweep of the beautiful, self-absorbed solo in the second act. The role was originally created for Antoinette Sibley, a superb classical dancer with a fabled technique but with neither the dramatic range nor intensity of expression of Lynn Seymour, whose qualities of movement the ballet so singularly evoked. One had the curious sensation on the first night of seeing a second performance from a different ballerina than the one who created it.

Lynn was competing with the memories of Natalia Makarova, who had danced the role before her. It was interesting to see again how a major role can be viewed from new angles when performed by the greatest of expressive artists. In the opening scene her Manon was mercenary, almost hard-bitten, a young girl who was determined not to be poor; while Makarova gave us a portrait of innocence caught up almost against her will, by the allure of riches and glittering jewels. Makarova showed a surface depravity beneath an essential innocence; Lynn Seymour, a surface innocence beneath a more fundamental depravity. The one was drawn by the blaze of diamonds, the brilliance of lit rooms; the other by a need for wealth as a means towards security, by men because of the demands of her own sensuality. It may be that Lynn Seymour is closer to Prévost's novel, although perhaps Makarova is nearer to MacMillan's vision. The dancing in each case was superb. Lynn Seymour belonged to those great duets, so richly coloured by her own individual style of movement, dances that had awaited her coming, anticipating her even during their composition.

Like Natalia Makarova before her, she reached one of the great peaks of her career in the wonderful last *pas de deux* when Manon, all her shrillness and frivolity gone, is enfolded in the final solemnity of death. It is one of MacMillan's most profound compositions where the dance achieves piercing intensity, but only great dancers can reach such icy pinnacles of expressive art.

During this season Lynn and Natalia Makarova shared the leading roles: two great ballerinas, quite different in physique and style, yet with so much in common as interpretative artists. As Marcia Haydée had also been a guest with the Royal Ballet, audiences at Covent Garden have had the amazing good fortune to compare the three greatest expressive dancers in the world in dramatic roles. They are all of nearly the same age, all at the height of their powers; and one would have to search deep into the history of the dance to find a parallel. They are very different in approach. Lynn Seymour is so near to life and the contemporary world; she is to the dance what Colette is to the novel. No artist invokes the world of physical sensation as she is able to do: the heat of the day and of loving, the loneliness and the atrocious grief at love's end. Haydée is the perfect example of what Ninette de Valois has described as the tense dancer. There is something hawk-like about her as she pounces on the musical phrase with that coiled intensity she gives to every movement. If she is the dancer of fire, both in the spiritual and physical sense, Natalia Makarova is the dancer of air, of the spirit seen through the flesh. She can create visionary landscapes, while Lynn Seymour makes us see the hills and valleys of the living earth. Lynn Seymour looks up at the stars, but Makarova can look beyond them.

In February 1976 Lynn appeared in Hans van Manen's masterly little duet, *Twilight*—a bitter, cruel sexual battle, set in the disfigured urban streets of our destroyed cities. Here she found a coarse rapaciousness, a shallow cruelty and a greediness for love that was, as the choreographer must have intended, both of our time and timeless. Here was the world of the disco and the cheap *palais de danse*, the hamburger on the late bus home, lovers crumpled together in small, mean rooms. Her performance brought to mind the indifferent lovelessness, the dull ache of dissatisfied sexuality of *The Waste Land*:

> *When lovely woman stoops to folly and*
> *Paces about her room again, alone,*
> *She smoothes her hair with automatic hand,*
> *And puts a record on the gramophone.*

During this extraordinarily creative period in her life Lynn was working again with Sir Frederick Ashton on his new

---

*In her famous role as Natalia Petrovna in Sir Frederick Ashton's ballet based on Turgenev's play,* A Month in the Country, *created for the Royal Ballet in 1976.*

ballet, *A Month in the Country*, first performed at Covent Garden on 12th February 1976 and his first major work since *Enigma Variations* eight years previously. It is a ballet of superb craftsmanship, even if at times one feels a certain lack of dramatic force in the images and in the structural development of the narrative. Of Lynn Seymour's performance one can have no reservations: in its variety of expression, the marvellous timing of gesture that could denote in a flash a new thought or feeling, the gentle, Mozartian sense of despair towards its close, she reaffirmed her place as one of the greatest of all dance-actresses in ballet.

Her dances had been most lovingly composed for her by Sir Frederick, much as one feels that later Antony Tudor was to create those exquisite dances that would suit no other for Gelsey Kirkland in *The Leaves are Fading* as a kind of beautiful, airy dress for her to wear. Clearly Ashton loved Lynn's style of dancing so much that he created a role to suit it perfectly, rather than discover—and if necessary force—new qualities of movement latent within her to achieve his own vision; this is perhaps why *A Month in the Country* lacks dramatic intensity.

Before the first performance Lynn awoke at midnight scarcely able to breathe. Pleurisy was suspected. She was X-rayed the next morning and spent the afternoon resting at the home of the Company's doctor. Then she went on to give one of the most remarkable performances of her life.

She met Dorothy Tutin who was playing the same role at the same time in a stage version of *A Month in the Country*. Tutin acts as Lynn Seymour dances; she phrases her words as Lynn phrases the music. For each of them the music of their different languages is the means through which their emotions speak with refinement and truth. In their different ways they are unique. All poetry, all expression in dance and in acting depends on timing and phrasing over which they have masterly and instinctive control, in which emotion is carried over tiny silences whose stillness bridges huge depths.

---

*A confrontation between Natalia and her ward, played by Denise Nunn, at the moment before she is slapped by Natalia, in* A Month in the Country.

As a little light relief Lynn presented the *Evening Standard* Ballet Award to her friend, Robert Cohen, Director of the London Contemporary Dance Theatre, in a delightful, witty speech that mentioned how his charm is such that he even managed to get Mr Bernard Levin into tights.

Then on 8th March Lynn was in Los Angeles to take part in a gala performance for Ballet Theatre. An astounding array of celebrated dancers had been gathered for the occasion; they included Alicia Alonso, Natalia Makarova, Marcia Haydée, Gelsey Kirkland, Mikhail Baryshnikov, Ivan Nagy, Richard Cragun and Fernando Bujones. Top prices were two hundred and fifty dollars—not much for such a blaze of stars. She danced the second movement *pas de deux* from *Concerto*, partnered by Gail Young, and her Isadora waltz, here entitled *Homage to Isadora*, accompanied by no less a person than Vladimir Ashkenazy. Although she had not met him before, Lynn personally invited Ashkenazy, a friend of Christopher Gable, to accompany the performance. With typical modesty he accepted, although he did not wish to appear on stage. Lynn recalls how he told her that he had never played the Opus 39 waltz, inquiring rather anxiously if she thought it was difficult. The *Los Angeles Times*, after praising her 'faintly overripe sensuality and just the right aura of rapturous abandon', ended the notice with the delightful remark: 'Eat your heart out, Vanessa Redgrave.'

The Royal Ballet opened its fifteenth tour of the United States in April at the Metropolitan Opera House. Lynn shared the leading roles in *Manon* and *Romeo and Juliet* with Natalia Makarova and gave her first performance in New York of *A Month in the Country* where it won universal acclaim. One of the New York critics wrote of 'the re-emergence of Lynn Seymour as a superlative interpretive dancer'. The critic continues:

> She has not been seen with the Royal Ballet in America for four years; she went through a very bad patch of overweight and under employment. Now she is back, wisp-like and totally fulfilling the promise she had as one of the great dancers of our time.

During this tour Lynn gave her first guest performances with the American Ballet Theatre at the Metropolitan Opera

House, New York, dancing in *Giselle* and Tudor's *Romeo and Juliet*. She was warmly welcomed both by the press and public alike; one critic found her performance in *Giselle* remarkable for the dramatic continuity of her playing, while in appearance she reminded him of certain photographs of Anna Pavlova in the role. Tudor's version of *Romeo and Juliet*, set to music by Delius, is a gentle, impressionistic meditation on the characters, made with rare subtlety and far removed from the high drama of the versions by MacMillan and Cranko with which she was familiar.

Public acknowledgement for Lynn's services to ballet came when she was awarded the CBE in the Birthday Honours in June 1976. Her recognition as a major artist was now complete and unequivocal and she may well have recalled with nostalgia that first *Swan Lake* in Melbourne eighteen years previously, when the Canadian flag flew over the theatre.

But the great occasion of the summer was the gala performance at Sadler's Wells to mark the fiftieth anniversary of Ballet Rambert on 15th June. Dame Marie Rambert was applauded from the moment she got out of her car outside the theatre until she took her seat, the whole house rising. Lynn danced her Isadora Duncan Waltzes as Ashton's tribute to her, since Duncan was one of the idols of Dame Marie's youth and together with Anna Pavlova, the inspiration for her life's work.

July saw her at the Coliseum, dancing with Nureyev in what was becoming his annual season there. She has always loved appearing with him, since his huge vitality and commitment to the dance are so much in accord with her own temperament. They danced in *Apollo*, in José Limón's *The Moor's Pavane* (where she was Desdemona to his Othello), in Paul Taylor's *Aureole* and in the big show-piece the *Corsaire pas de deux*, complete with *fouettés*—now no longer a nightmare to her. These had been added to the traditional choreography of the *pas de deux* by Nureyev in order to strengthen these for her return to *Swan Lake*, which she was to dance with the American Ballet Theatre in the State Theatre, New York in the autumn. Rudolf Nureyev helped her enormously with the role, which she had not danced for several years; but when she did appear in it with Ballet Theatre, to her horror the *fouettés*, which she had now so happily mastered, let her down during performance. She had seldom been so nervous before a major role and it seemed to her at the time as if the merciless gods had deliberately tampered with her execution of the *fouettés* on such a great and important occasion. She was shattered. There seemed no justice in the whole world; this was a particular torment reserved for ballerinas—especially guest artists on their opening night.

In addition to *Swan Lake* she danced in *Concerto* and most significantly of all, in Tudor's *Pillar of Fire*, where the role of Hagar was created by her friend, Nora Kaye, in 1942. It brought back memories of how Nora Kaye had recognised her potential in *The Invitation* sixteen years earlier.

During rehearsals Tudor seemed to despair of her even being able to dance the role, abandoning her for the four last days to work it out alone. He said he doubted if she would ever be able to do it, muttering dark threats about cancelling the performance. This was probably only tactical to bring out the best in her, since Tudor is a past master at conducting a war of nerves on his ballerinas. But it worked beautifully as it always seems to do with dancers in his ballets who, although reduced to the edge of a nervous breakdown by his various psychological manoeuvres, in the end—either in a blaze of anger or with the urgings of near despair—produce wonderful performances for him. So it was with *Pillar of Fire*, in which Lynn's interpretation was so assured, so individual that he even had the audacity to reprove her afterwards for pretending she was unable to dance it. Everyone who has worked with Tudor admires his genius, although sometimes during rehearsals they carry murder in their hearts.

Lynn found it very difficult to obtain the key to the character of Hagar but discovered it at last in a sense of social alienation. In this way she was able to link the role with the emotions she herself had felt when she first came to London, isolated both by her background and her accent from the class-structured society in which she found herself. It is essential, she says, to find such a key to unlock the imagination; after this the role becomes real to her own emotional life and she has a foundation on which to build. Sometimes it may be a very small thing. When, for example, she puzzled about the interpretation of the eldest sister in *Las Hermanas*, she recalled a gesture of Miss Edwards, when in moments of stress or anxiety she would pat her hair with one hand, setting it meticulously in shape. This gave her the key

*Lynn Seymour CBE with her children, the twins Jerszy and Adrian, and her younger son, Demian, outside Buckingham Palace.*

and from this she was able to grasp the nature of the character as a whole. In the same way she was able to identify the character of Manon with her demand for money as a means towards personal security, recalling in her own mind those early days as a student at Sadler's Wells, when she struggled to save a few pounds a month and ice cream was a dangerous extravagance.

Curious journalists wondered how she coped with it all: a home, a family, the continual pressure of new roles and guest appearances abroad. It might have seemed more difficult now

than ever, since she had to combine the problems of managing a great career and three merry children on her own (she and her husband had separated that year). In fact she managed beautifully. Lynn's friends all affirm that she is a wonderful mother, warm, loving and reasonable, treating her children as individuals with their own point of view that should be respected. The atmosphere at her home is one of joyful chaos. As she told an interviewer at this time:

> You make it sound like the Second World War. Having the children around helps me. I only get frazzled occasionally. They're marvellous to come home to. I feel sorry for mothers who have to stick at home with the kids all day. I think it's nice for the children that I'm not here all the time. I'd become a bore. This way when we see each other we see each other fresh.

After a season with the Touring Company at Sadler's Wells she danced at Covent Garden in the first performance by the Royal Ballet of Glen Tetley's masterpiece, *Voluntaries*, which was created as his tribute to John Cranko. This superb work affirms the triumph of the creative spirit over death, as Cranko had triumphed; in a wider sense it is an allegory of the primal myth of rebirth through suffering. Lynn's performance was one of absolute classical simplicity. While the richness in style was as apparent as ever, it had been reduced to its essentials, to images of great purity and refinement. It was noble, tragic, impassioned; but it was also a statement of beautiful reserve, one remarkable in a dancer in many ways so outspoken in movement. It is true she could not give the role the same personal feeling as Marcia Haydée, for whom it was composed; but Haydée was one of Cranko's dearest friends and she danced the work with his memory still green, still beloved, much as years earlier Margot Fonteyn had performed *Tiresias* to Constant Lambert's music with incredible dedication and for her friend so recently dead. Haydée had something within her that neither Lynn Seymour

---

*Lynn dances at a gala performance in a rare* pas de trois *from* The Corsair, *revived by Rudolf Nureyev.*

*With David Wall in Glen Tetley's* Voluntaries, *composed originally for the Stuttgart ballet in 1973 as a memorial to its founder and choreographer, John Cranko, who died that year. It was presented by the Royal Ballet at Covent Garden in 1976.*

194

nor Natalia Makarova, who alternated in the role, could be expected to share.

Despite the enormous pressure of work Lynn remained serene and perhaps more assured than at any time in her life. Her career had begun to take a new direction as a choreographer and the year 1976 ended in optimism, not, like so many others in the past, on a note of despondency and apprehension about the future.

After these two triumphant years, the pinnacle of her career to date, she now arrived at a plateau which as time passed she began to notice was once more, in the dreaded pattern, beginning to slope downhill. There had been highlighs (the *Evening Standard* award for Ballet in April; performances in *Les Sylphides* with Makarova and Fonteyn during Nureyev's Coliseum season in the summer; the making of her first film *Leda and the Swan* for BBC television, and a new role in MacMillan's Jubilee piece, *Gloriana*) but the shadows were beginning to gather again. The big new roles did not materialise. John Neumeier's *The Fourth Symphony*, first performed at Covent Garden in March 1977, gave her scant opportunities as an expressive artist; while the production of *Onegin*, probably John Cranko's finest work with a marvellous role for her, had to be abandoned owing to technical difficulties about fire-proofing for the sets. It was maddening, since the replacement ballet—Cranko's *The Taming of the Shrew*—was a far inferior work in which she had little opportunity to extend her range either as a dancer or an actress, even though she created a delightful termagant, a mass of quivering suspicion and hostility whose drooping submission at the end still contained more than a hint of sharp but hidden claws.

The outstanding event for her during 1977 was a new production of *The Sleeping Beauty* by Ninette de Valois at Covent Garden in which she was cast as the wicked fairy, Carabosse, and painted a portrait of gloating evil, edged by a crooked smile. In the intervals between acts she took the opportunity to rehearse the role of Aurora with Rudolf Nureyev, since she was to dance it later in the season. It was a rapid transformation—a matter, she says, merely of whipping off one's wig and beginning the famous dances and duets, while the stage staff worked in the background. Those snatched few minutes between acts were to prove of immense

*As Carabosse in Dame Ninette de Valois' production of* The Sleeping Beauty, *Covent Garden, 1977.*

value to her when she appeared for the first time as Aurora with Nureyev in this new production on 2nd November, still with the same youthful radiance, the sense of a young girl on the brink of life for whom the *rose adagio* is an adventure of the heart as well as a study in pure classicism.

Nureyev's personal involvement in her performances was so close that she recalls one occasion when, quite overcome by her dancing of Aurora, he wandered out on stage from his place in the wings, returning there after this dreamy perambulation, seemingly unaware of his unchoreographed appearance. Some members of the audience must have been somewhat taken aback by his arrival, which did not seem wholly to be in accord with their programme notes.

196

The first two months of 1978 were crowded with engagements, although this was to be the last busy period she was to have. She danced in Nureyev's version of *Romeo and Juliet* both in London with the Festival Ballet and at the Palais des Sports in Paris. She also appeared in *La Sylphide* with Ruth Page's Chicago Ballet in Chicago, partnered by Peter Schaufuss, now no longer reluctant to dance with him as she had been when he was fourteen years old.

Her major role, however, was that of Mary Vetsera in Kenneth MacMillan's *Mayerling*, first performed at Covent Garden on 14th February. Again MacMillan had sought to investigate an historical mystery: the strange double deaths of Crown Prince Rudolf of Austria and his mistress, Mary Vetsera, in the hunting lodge at Mayerling, a subject for endless speculation and the theme of a celebrated film with Garbo. MacMillan has a unique quality of being able to suggest the most complex emotional states in movement— particularly in *pas de deux*, some of which were more erotic, more daring in their lifts and original in their invention than any he had composed before. It is like a landscape, suddenly transformed into eerie and terrible beauty by flashes of lightning. To these, as in a beautiful drifting solo earlier in the ballet, he gave Lynn Seymour huge scope for delicate musical phrasing on the one hand and savage, almost rapacious sexuality on the other. It was difficult for her to develop the character and she found little in the role to stimulate her imagination. Mary Vetsera does not appear until near the middle of the ballet; nothing really prepares one for the impassioned duets in which she is involved. Lynn made of the role what she could; the sensuality of her dancing had the shameless abandon of a girl recklessly and wantonly in love. To show this in movement is where the genius of MacMillan as a choreographer resides; nowhere in his other ballets are the self-destructive passions exposed, nerve by nerve, in such nakedness or with so dark and troubled an imagination.

Despite its flaw in dramatic structure and balance, *Mayerling* contains solo dances for all the principal artists in which the complex, and often ambiguous relationships between the characters are explored with great subtlety. He searches their inner lives, the darkest reaches of the unconscious. These solos were like an inner reverie in which emotions shift, collide and reform in a manner that leads to no resolution, only to the

Mayerling *by Kenneth MacMillan, first performed in 1978, showing the tragic love of Mary Vetsera for the Crown Prince Rudolf of Austria. Lynn is seen with David Wall in their created roles.*

most painful ambiguity and self-questioning. Here MacMillan has brought choreography closer to the art of the writer than any of his predecessors in terms of the analysis of unconscious motives.

The ballet showed in the clearest light yet both the strength and the weaknesses of MacMillan's work at full length: the sense of drama without an equal ability to sustain a dramatic narrative; the lack of balance between passages of the most intense imagining and those of dull, repetitive movement, particularly in group as opposed to solo dances and *pas de deux*; a certain inability to focus dramatic climaxes with real intensity, so that they appear either rather haphazard and insufficiently prepared for or clumsily placed within the narrative. In literary terms it is the art of a great short story writer extended to a novel for which a different technique is required and which, at the moment, MacMillan has not completely at his command. *Mayerling* looks at certain moments like a masterpiece; at others like a failure in both narrative and structure. It is, however, the work of a great choreographer who, one feels, has not yet found the subject where his extraordinary insight into the human heart discovers a structure adequate to contain it.

The spring tour of the United States by the Royal Ballet brought Lynn new acclaim for her performance in *Mayerling*, even though the ballet came in for a good deal of criticism. But on this tour something far more unexpected had occurred. One evening she was astonished to receive a telephone call from the Director of the Bavarian State Opera in Munich, offering her the appointment as artistic director of the ballet company there. Ever since her period with the Berlin Oper she had had a great reputation in Germany, where she is one of the most admired of all western ballerinas. Her new career as a choreographer was an added incentive, as was her prestige in Stuttgart, where she had danced as a guest artist several times. It was a big decision to make and she did not accept at once, but she was very tempted.

She considered the matter during her summer engagements, including the Commonwealth Dance Gala at Alberta (in which she danced the balcony *pas de deux* from *Romeo and Juliet*) and the 'Stars of the Ballet' season at the Festival Hall. These were rather dreary evenings of continual *pas de deux*, like a dinner consisting entirely of radishes.

A tour to Athens with the Royal Ballet followed, then dreaded routine took over again. She was limited during the winter season to a series of performances in *Mayerling* and *A Month in the Country*. Apart from a tiny work by David Bintley, *Take Five*, created to celebrate Dame Ninette's eightieth birthday, she had no new roles. She would continue, of course, to dance smaller roles as they returned to the repertoire, such as the Spring and Summer variations and adagios in MacMillan's *The Four Seasons*, or one of the Seasons in Ashton's *Cinderella*, but these were no real challenge to her. She was bored; she wanted a new challenge. It was too safe with the Royal Ballet. Nor does she much like to be kept waiting to see

*A* pas de trois *from a revived production of* Symphony, *to music by Shostakovitch, with Donald MacLeary and Wayne Eagling. The ballet was created by Kenneth MacMillan in 1963.*

what happens. She had done that before in 1966 and 1973, frustrated by an increasingly limited number of roles, and in the end she could wait no longer.

She decided to accept the offer from the Bavarian State Opera. She realised it was a big risk, indeed an almost impossible task to be the leading ballerina, a choreographer and director of the same company, but she has never feared what others fear is the near impossible. Like her grandfather who set up his forge on an empty landscape and saw it grow into a town, she wanted to be a pioneer as well, to build her own city.

Left, *Lynn and David Wall in* Mayerling.

# PART THREE

# 1: The Choreographer

LYNN SEYMOUR was first encouraged to test her gifts for choreography by Glen Tetley, who for many years has had huge admiration for her dancing. He felt that someone with such an instinctive feeling for creative movement might well have similar abilities as a choreographer. Her first apprentice works were performed at two Royal Ballet choreographic workshops in 1973 and 1974. Entitled *Night Ride* and *Breakthrough* they were based on a series of *pas de deux*; it has always been in the *pas de deux* that Lynn—like Fonteyn before her—has achieved the greatest artistic satisfaction as a dancer. She knew that Kenneth MacMillan usually began a work by constructing a *pas de deux*, whatever place it finally took in the completed ballet; in one of his greatest works, for example, *Song of the Earth*, the first section he choreographed was in fact the duet in the last scene. MacMillan was the model from whom she chose to work.

She had only choreographed one piece before this—a dance in the style of Isadora Duncan to music by Scriabin which Clement Crisp had encouraged her to compose for herself at a lecture demonstration they had earlier given together, when he had wished to contrast classical and modern techniques in ballet. It is interesting that her most famous solo, *Five Dances in the Manner of Isadora Duncan*, was to be created for her by Frederick Ashton only a couple of years later.

The theme of *Night Ride* was inspired by a story told to her by Frank Frey, her young partner in Berlin. He was travelling on the overnight train to Copenhagen to see his girlfriend; in the same compartment was a girl on her way to see her boyfriend. They began to talk, to fall in love; then they parted and went their separate ways. The score was written by a very talented young composer, Michael Finnissy. Lynn thought it best to start her career with a duet and she composed a moving, rather sad little *pas de deux* that Kenneth MacMillan liked when he saw it. He therefore encouraged her to go a step further; this time she should include a group of dancers as well as a pair of soloists.

This second ballet, *Breakthrough*, is the story of a girl finding true love—a very romantic piece told in a modern manner. The score was again by Michael Finnissy and played by the London Sinfonietta. As MacMillan had advised, she used a small group of boys from the Rambert school as a *corps de ballet.*

From these cautious beginnings she joined forces with Robert North, already an established choreographer with the London Contemporary Dance Theatre and a friend of hers, to compose a work together. *Gladly, Sadly, Badly, Madly* was first performed in 1975 to a pop music score and was a real success. It was a duet for a pair of young lovers, set at night amid the swirling mist, where they are first seen sitting on a bench. There follows a series of *pas de deux*, relating to the different moods of the title, nicely composed with some beautiful lifts. This is certainly not Aurora, whom Lynn Seymour was by now beginning actively to dislike; this was a shopgirl, a hat-check girl in a night club or a bored typist spending each week in some ghastly city office, finding love and some living under an appropriate urban moon. The atmosphere is much nearer to the spirit of van Manen, whose ballets—such as *Twilight* and *Tilt*—are so vividly imagined with a sardonic but compassionate understanding, full of the glare of neon, cheap music and the misty glow of lights in anonymous cities. From Robert North she learned a good deal about how to compose a ballet, so that she could approach her own first professional work with more confidence. She and North were awarded a scholarship from the Royal Society of Arts and the Leverhulme Trust for this ballet, which allowed them an opportunity for further study in the United States.

As Kenneth MacMillan had discovered a girl in the *corps de ballet* who was to be his inspiration, so Lynn Seymour chose a little known young dancer for the lead in both of these ballets. She had been struck by the fluidity of movement, the sensual quality of the dancing and the dramatic intensity of June Highwood, a beautiful girl with the same whimsical, gamine and expressive face as the young Seymour.

*Lynn Seymour's first ballet,* Rashomon *(1976), contained impassioned duets for June Highwood and her two partners, Desmond Kelly* (seated) *and Robert North.*

It was for June Highwood, partnered by Robert North and Desmond Kelly, that Lynn Seymour created her first real work, *Rashomon*, with music by Bob Downes, performed by the Sadler's Wells Royal Ballet on 19th October 1976. The ballet was based on a film by Kurosawa that tells of a man, his wife and a passing marauder, who give three conflicting accounts about a nasty event, apparently a rape that took place in a wood. Lynn had again acted on MacMillan's advice to go to an existing story and attempt a work in narrative. She had seen a ballet on this theme in Berlin by Tatiana Gsovsky to music by Varèse and had been struck by the way in which she used a huge platform stage and filled it with stylised movement. For her first professional attempt she did not, however, wish to create anything so ambitious.

The superb sets for the ballet were by Pamela Marre, then one of Nicholas Georgiadis' students at the Slade School and later to achieve a similar triumph in design for Christopher Bruce's ballet *Night with Waning Moon* in 1979. It is interesting that Lynn first suggested the idea to the students as a design project before she was asked to create the ballet. She had great difficulty in composing the fights that occupy an important part of the work and studied the martial arts techniques of Japan at the Aikido Academy in London, from where one of the instructors came to advise the dancers.

She was, of course, fortunate to have June Highwood, who was already familiar with her style and methods of working, Robert North, and the hugely versatile Desmond Kelly to dance the three roles. She says with characteristic modesty that they practically did it all for her. The idea of the cowardly fight she discovered from her childhood, recalling two men, drunk after a convivial night, making ineffectual attempts to hit one another and pulling each other's hair, in the kitchen at home.

The ballet made a considerable impact, having genuine dramatic force and a unity between its components in the best traditions of the Fokine dance-drama. Glen Tetley saw it and was very impressed. The range of movement was not great, but the duets were extremely powerful and erotic, with the two bodies slithering over one another or glued together in fierce embrace. June Highwood, in particular, gave a tremendous performance in the difficult and tortuous *pas de deux* to which she brought a kind of sensual abandon that recalled Jeanmaire's legendary dancing in *Carmen*. The fights were well constructed but the little solo work was not very expressive. It was, however, a professional ballet and promised well for the future.

Her next ballet was a complete contrast. This was *The Court of Love*, performed by the same company at Sadler's Wells in their Jubilee season on 26th April 1977. It deals with Queen Eleanor of Aquitaine and her Renaissance court in Poitiers. It is little more than a series of *divertissements*, made to measure for a royal occasion and the sense of national euphoria created by the Jubilee. It was, however, composed at very short notice: Lynn had only three weeks to work on it before the first performance. Because of the demand for dancers in other works, she was also obliged to use a number of quite inexperienced artists, some with little stage experience. The idea for the ballet came from the composer of the music, Howard Blake. Lynn wanted something light, festive and with royal connections as befitted the time, and a medieval court seemed the ideal setting. The designs were by Dimitra

Maraslis, another of Georgiadis' students from the Slade; unfortunately through lack of time his splendid Gothic set was incomplete and not well reproduced.

The ballet was designed around three contrasted episodes in which the ladies were courted, with interruptions by comic solos for three knaves and a sextet of demure angels who decorated the stage very prettily. It contains one elegant *pas de deux* in the classical manner and elaborate groupings. As a *pièce d'occasion* it worked well, but had not the staying power to remain for long in the repertoire. Robert Helpmann who was a guest artist with the touring company, much admired the ballet, telling her that had it been produced twenty years earlier it would have caused a sensation.

Her third creation, *Intimate Letters*, was first performed at Sadler's Wells on 10th October 1978. Here she reverted to the type of dance drama perfected by Tudor in *Jardin aux Lilas* and *Pillar of Fire*; and it may be that her experience of dancing in *Pillar of Fire* with Ballet Theatre had coloured her imagination, since there are certain similarities in style and the quality of movement. It is brilliantly conceived in terms of theatre in that the musicians for Janacek's second string quartet are on stage, entertaining at a party that takes place around them. The choreographer had the very original idea of mixing taped conversation and laughter between each movement. This works marvellously, giving a sense of reality to the ballet, the feeling of one certain evening never to be repeated, emotions that existed and merged on that night only, that one finds so incomparably expressed in *Jardin aux Lilas*, the first and probably the greatest of all ballets in this style.

The story is partly biographical in the sense that she has used experiences and relationships of her own life in an imaginative manner, interposing fact and fiction; even the twins appear with their mother. The ballet is dedicated to the memory of John Gale, who figures as one of the protagonists in the work. Lynn had the advantage of a well constructed narrative, for which she owed much to Gillian Freeman who devised it; and the complex relationships between the mother, her husband, the man she loves and the man who loves her are explored with real dramatic skill, the dances flowing in the best Tudor manner.

The taped conversations were made by Albert Finney and Sara Kestelman of the National Theatre in a curious amalgam

*Galina Samsova as The Woman and David Ashmole as The Man she loves in Lynn Seymour's third ballet,* Intimate Letters, *created for the Sadler's Wells Royal Ballet in 1978.*

of 'rhubarb' and Czech that worked so well that the tape did not have to be edited at all, although Bob Downes combined it with other sounds in a masterly fashion. Sara Kestelman and a very talented theatrical director from Australia, Rodney Fisher, attended many rehearsals since Lynn was determined the work should be genuinely theatrical in form. She has always seen ballet as a dramatic art in a wider context than that of the dance; the ideas of those outside the rather narrow world of ballet thus did much to enrich the work.

Much of the success of the ballet was due to the wonderful performance by Galina Samsova in the main role, where her warmth, subtlety of expression and dramatic intensity brought conviction to the limited range of images she had to dance. In her anxiety to avoid the overdramatic Lynn Seymour understated the dance so that it lacked real expressive force in its imagery, which carried little emotional weight.

For the part of a young rival Lynn chose Siobhàn Stanley, who brought true feeling to a small role, giving it a bright, rather cruel intensity that gave additional balance to the work. Siobhàn Stanley is now, together with the brilliantly gifted Nicola Katrak, one of the most exciting talents of the new generation of dancers in the Royal Ballet.

It is too early to know how or even if Lynn Seymour will develop as a choreographer. Certainly, the sense of drama, of ballet as a structural whole, involving décor and lighting as well as dance, is there; how far she will be able to forge her own style remains to be seen. The two light, cabaret-type pieces based on *The Threepenny Opera* that she composed for gala ballet seasons at the Festival Hall in 1978 and 1979 are merely amusing and ephemeral and tell us very little about her talent. Kenneth MacMillan, Dame Ninette de Valois and Sir Frederick Ashton have all helped her with their advice; but in the last analysis, choreographers—the rarest of all artists in ballet—are like poets, born not made.

Lynn has a very down-to-earth attitude towards her choreography. She says:

> I am still a beginner. I don't take myself too
> seriously as a choreographer yet. I mean, you can't,
> not having worked with people like MacMillan,
> Ashton and Balanchine. But I hope to keep on
> learning.

MacMillan, however, is sure of her gifts as a choreographer, agreeing that this is an inborn talent which cannot be learned. He says:

> I think she is enormously talented. I don't think,
> however, that she will ever really develop into a
> great choreographer until she gives up dancing. At
> the moment she is pulled two ways: she wants to be
> a dancer, and she wants to be a choreographer. I
> don't think (except in very rare cases) you can be
> both. You have to sacrifice a lot to be a
> choreographer.

She has a number of ideas stored away in notebooks and she is not discouraged by the cool reception given to her first ballets by most of the critics. It is a perilous and difficult art. She has never been one to avoid a challenge of this nature.

# 2: Artistic Director

HE YEAR Lynn spent as artistic director of the Bavarian State Ballet was the most exhausting, exasperating and, at rare times, the most fulfilling of any in her career. She now looks back on it with a kind of bemused amazement; in some ways it was too astounding to be true.

When she arrived, the authorities at the Opera House did not exactly lay out the red carpet for her; it was more like a rug that could be pulled from under her feet with the greatest dexterity. She had no secretary, no staff and in trying to rectify the matter, she encountered a bureaucratic structure of almost Byzantine inscrutability. Negotiations continued for months. In the meantime she was obliged to write all her letters by hand, often working a twenty-hour day. Departmental heads and financial committees loomed above her, while even to discover who was responsible for any particular problem meant an in-depth investigation among an administrative staff of twelve hundred responsible for running the Opera, each deeply enmeshed in committes of various kinds. There was also a staff association, known as the *Buhnengenossenschaft*—enough to terrify anyone. While struggling within the bureaucratic web Lynn had also to fulfil her engagements with the Royal Ballet in *Mayerling*, *Anastasia* and *The Concert* at Covent Garden. The twins remained in London, joining her and Demian for the holidays.

Morale among the dancers was low since the ballet, as with most opera houses on the continent, was treated not so much as a poor relation of the opera but as a kind of impoverished country cousin, useful only on those few nights—at the most five a month—when the opera company was not performing.

It carried a fine repertoire of full length ballets, many of them the heritage from the years John Cranko worked with the Company. These included the main classics, *Swan Lake*, *The Sleeping Beauty* and *Giselle*; Cranko's full-length ballets, *Romeo and Juliet*, *Onegin* and *The Taming of the Shrew*, together with Ashton's *La Fille Mal Gardée*. There was a conspicuous lack of any modern, short ballets, since the idea of a mixed triple bill was not acceptable to Munich audiences unless it could be devoted to a single composer.

The dancers came from all over the world, making a polyglot company drawn from many schools and with a variety of styles. There were, among others, dancers from England, Germany, Hungary, Czechoslovakia, Yugoslavia, Japan, Iceland and the United States. The dancers seemed to run things much as they pleased, the company being roughly structured on the traditional lines of principals, soloists and *corps de ballet*. These lines, Lynn found when she sought to promote talented younger dancers, were drawn with very strong definition.

The Opera House itself is grand, not to say grandiloquent, with five tiers and a vast chandelier. Large caryatids flank the Royal Box. The auditorium holds some two thousand, with a wider stage than Covent Garden, marvellously equipped with mechanical and electronic aids. It is ideal for ballet, lacking only a ballet company with a coherent style and a varied repertoire to complete it.

Lynn was very much aware of the lack of modern ballets in the repertoire, so that she decided to offer as her début a programme of works new to her audience. This triple bill would be made up of her own ballet, *Intimate Letters*, with Galina Samsova as guest artist; Harold Lander's *Etudes*, a fine work in the repertoire of many companies but not previously seen in Munich and in which Peter Schaufuss would appear, and a new ballet by a talented young choreographer, Youri Vamos, a dancer in the company. She had less than two months in which to prepare this evening. She knew that choreographers first establish a style, and a school then secures it. This was how both the Vic-Wells Ballet and Ballet Rambert had charted their progress in the early days; and since she was fortunate enough to have a young choreographer among her dancers, she would follow the same plan. The school was a long-term objective, essential to her design, but this could not be established overnight. She set about mounting this first

210

programme with great enthusiasm. The public was not to share it.

The first and only night of this triple bill was not, to put it mildly, a success. This was not due to the quality of the works, since *Etudes* is a fine and well-established ballet, while *Intimate Letters*, although no masterpiece, did not meet any such hostility from the far more experienced audiences at Sadler's Wells. It was, in fact, prejudice, well organised in advance, well orchestrated in the theatre. They did not want her as artistic director, even though they did not really know whom they wanted; they did not want her as their ballerina. Now was the time to show it. They booed and whistled and laughed throughout much of the evening; at the end the cacophony was quite frightening.

At once the press joined in. The performance was described by one paper as 'a scandal'; another said, 'Now ballet has become something to laugh at.' Only the *Frankfurter Allgemeine Zeitung* came to Lynn's rescue, describing the reception as 'breaking the laws of hospitality and fair play'. One critic even took exception to the fact that Lynn was described in a programme note as a *prima ballerina* and asked for proof, as if the evidence had not been on display in opera houses throughout the western world for some fifteen years. The quality of the fare set before this irate and vociferous section of the public was, in fact, irrelevant; all that concerned them was their determination to smash the crockery. This they did with gusto, leaving the unfortunate artistic director to sweep up the pieces.

'Nothing daunted' is easily said, but she certainly did not sit among the wreckage and wring her hands. On 16th December, some two weeks later, she was to make her first appearance in John Cranko's *Romeo and Juliet.* Marcia Haydée came across from Stuttgart to help with rehearsals and to give her additional coaching, just as she had encouraged her when they were both in their teens at the Sadler's Wells School some twenty-five years earlier. In addition Richard Craigun, one of the world's finest male dancers, was to partner her. Lynn needed their support. She had received twenty threatening and abusive letters, promising the maximum hostility towards her on the night.

The performance was in fact a triumph, not only artistically but in terms of character. The public and critics were forced to eat their words and they did so with as much dignity as they could muster. The Munich *Abendzeitung* said that her performance:

> possesses a touching naturalness which swamps all the high-bred artificialities of ballet. She transforms choreographic steps into a spiritual experience ... her dance style is the very enemy of pose, turgidity and of stylised dishonesty.

The more vocal of her critics sat back on their heels and waited in gloomy silence. Further support then came from her friends Natalia Makarova and Rudolf Nureyev who appeared as her first guest artists in *Swan Lake*. It would hardly be possible to excel that and the existing hostility was to a large extent muffled.

Slowly Lynn began to find her way through the bureaucratic maze, even though she was severely restricted in her range of action. She had no budget, no control over any expenses. She could not engage either famous guest artists or a single dancer for the *corps de ballet* without seeking prior approval. Her idea of using distinguished guest teachers to raise the standard of dancing met with a blank refusal. She could not commission a designer. She could not even get a studio painted or a *barre* moved without approval from somewhere within the maze. She says:

> They had very little use for a director of ballet. No way could I make any final decision about policy without going through a whole layer of bureaucratic heads, most of whom had little or no knowledge of ballet.

Her fierce will and her sense of humour saved the day.

Most serious of all, she could find no support for the second part of her grand design. No progress could be made in establishing a school attached to the company, even though she had the promise of help with this from Dame Ninette de Valois and the situation was ideal. Apart from the ballet company at the Opera House there was a second company with its own separate organisation at the Teater am Gartnerplatz that presented evenings of ballet as well as operas—rather similar to the Opéra Comique in Paris and the Maly Ballet in Leningrad. It was common sense to suggest that both these companies should be served from the same school from which students could be drawn for walk-on parts in the opera, now being filled by dancers. She got nowhere—where she seemed so often to arrive after endless meetings—a somewhat barren spot for one of her determination.

Coupled with these problems, she was from March 1979, continually unwell and unable to dance, so that in the summer she was obliged to return to London for an operation, cancelling her scheduled performances at the Festival Hall. Even so she had achieved a great deal: a Bournonville evening was presented, including a performance of *La Sylphide* with Joyce Cuoco—formerly with the Stuttgart Company—as the Sylph and Lynn herself having enormous fun as Madge the witch. During the ballet week she mounted a gala performance of new ballets by her own choreographer, Youri Vamos, John Neumeier, William Forsythe and herself. She revived her own *Rashomon* and mounted a new production of Kenneth MacMillan's *Las Hermanas*, long out of the repertoire of the company. She presented a choreographic workshop in which no less than six new pieces by members of the company were shown.

In addition to this she sought to improve the structure of the company itself. An administrative staff had been formed, a new ballet master engaged, young dancers nursed into leading roles. One of these, Louise Lester, trained at the Royal Ballet School, danced a first Aurora of great promise. Three different casts were established for the big works, something unheard of in the past. By midsummer, when she returned to London for her operation, she could look back with a sense of real achievement, even though it fell far short of what she had at first envisaged.

But now, unable to dance and with a period of convalescence ahead, the main objectives of a school, a separate budget and powers of decision on matters that affected the company still not allowed her, she felt no purpose would be served in continuing. If the goals had been attainable, she could try again; but they were not, and would never be until those in authority realised that a ballet company must run as a coherent entity and not as an off-shoot of the opera.

It was not worth risking her career as a dancer any further, to endanger the happiness of her children, who had not liked the long separations both from her and from one another. Very amicably it was agreed she would not extend her contract beyond the end of 1979. She will continue to advise her successor, to give him or her all the help they need, but now, blinking in the unexpected light of a brilliant London autumn, she has her own future to consider. At least she has left things in better order than she found them. It was all she could have done.

# PART FOUR

# 1: The Ballerina

ORDS MAY FAIL US, music may not reach us, but the dance will speak to the most enclosed heart. Of all the arts it is the most accessible—a shared world of beautiful images, more immediate than words and nearer than music; one that speaks in terms of our common humanity, even of our most secret inner lives, known to us only in our dreams.

The purest aspect of the dance is the classical ballet, since it combines the greatest visual beauty with an emotional content that has been intensified by the very limitations of its form. The classical technique is a kind of burning glass of our emotional life: by limiting its range, it intensifies its brightness, so that emotions are compressed into their essences, stripped bare of all that might diminish or impede them. An artist, whether poet or dancer, must be bounded— like Hamlet—in a nutshell in order to find himself king of infinite spaces.

The dancer is in a strange position: she is both near to us in her humanity and distanced from us by her technique. The impersonality of the structure of the classical dance allows the humanity of the dancer to reach us in a manner that is unique in theatrical art. She is like us, mortal and imperfect, yet she speaks to us in a language that is timeless and universal, a world of images and symbols that lie deep within our unconscious. Her task is to communicate to us an allegory of her inner world, seen through a choreographer's vision, so that we can recognise truths which cannot be known in any other language but the dance. Few dancers have been able to achieve this, although it is the aim of all their endeavours. One of these is Lynn Seymour.

There are certain qualities that all great dancers hold in common. The most important of these is sincerity. A great dancer does not cheat; she does not seek to deceive her audience, either by a faked technique or with false emotions. She communicates in her dancing what her heart tells her and what her instinct confirms as being a meeting point between herself and the role she portrays on the stage. This is sometimes called personality, temperament, or 'star quality'; but this encounter between an artist's inner world and its outward projection in the theatre is more elusive.

A theatrical performance is, of course, an artifice. It is, in one sense, an unreal world, constructed of plywood and coloured lights and all the other deceptions of the stage. Rare artists bring to this artifice their own humanity; a ballet like *Giselle* is not just a quaint period drama of love and deceit, it is also the recollection of their own loving, their experiences of defeat, the death of love as they have known it in their own lives. This is what made Anna Pavlova so great a dancer and one so loved: in all the generosity of her spirit she shared with her audience the whole drama of her inner life—her moods, her moments of childlike joy, her insecurities and her hidden fears. These she was able to present in dances, often of hopeless triviality but into which she poured the richness of her spirit and so transformed them. And so it is also with Lynn Seymour, in many ways a stronger, more secure and balanced personality than the great ballerinas who have preceded her or with whom she shares the stage today.

What places her in this rare company is the same refusal to conceal her real self behind the artifices of the theatre. She gives the whole of herself, the commitment of her whole personality, to the dance. 'To write is to hand oneself over,' said François Mauriac, and a great dancer does the same. This humanity makes Lynn Seymour a superb dramatic dancer, bringing immediacy to every performance. It is not 'emotion recollected in tranquillity', but emotion lived with the same vividness as it was first experienced, linking her personal life to her stage creations without the sense of artifice or strain. It is typical of her that the gesture of grief, made by the young Anastasia in Kenneth MacMillan's ballet, in which she tucks both hands in her armpits, was taken straight from a gesture she often made in anger or sadness as a child, to enclose herself and to form a barrier against the outside world.

*The 'mad scene' in* Giselle, *from a television production with Rudolf Nureyev and the Bavarian State Opera Ballet on New Year's Eve, 1979.*

Because Lynn Seymour is outgoing by temperament, generous and liable to impulsive kindnesses as well as to unpredictable storms, she is sometimes inclined to give too much as a dancer. Roles that require great restraint, either because they must retain a sense of period, such as *Giselle*, or because their emotions are touched on very lightly, such as *Les Sylphides*, often seem to make her impatient. Similarly, her sense of fun is unequalled and she is the most brilliant comedienne on the contemporary ballet stage; but sometimes she overdoes it, gets carried away by her own involvement in the joke, too eager to share it with her audience. These are faults of a largesse of spirit, and not the sort of meanness that will short-change an audience and give them no more than they deserve, which is the failing of some other dancers. Lynn Seymour is loved because her performances are like a gift which she presents to her audience without any self-consciousness or desire to be loved by them, only because it is in her nature as an artist to give, even, if necessary, to excess. A remark she made to Peter Wright, Director of Sadler's Wells Royal Ballet, during a season at the Edinburgh Festival, sums up her attitude: 'Dancers should be so grateful for what they are. There is such a wealth of life in being a dancer.'

It is impossible to separate a dancer's style and technique from her personality. The openness of spirit, so characteristic of Lynn Seymour, is expressed in her dancing. Although she has danced for many years with the Royal Ballet, she has always had her own distinctive quality of movement. It has a soft, dreamy flow, where the images melt one into another in the eddies of the dance and at its close fade into the music with an exquisite finality. Dame Ninette de Valois sees the relationship between physique, style and temperament (which in Lynn Seymour's case owes much to her Scottish blood) as being so close as to be indivisible. Lynn is less reticent, less restrained in approach than her English colleagues. She is from the New World, of the New World, whose restless and adventurous spirit she carries over into her dancing. Dame Ninette sees her as the Isadora Duncan of our times—the daring and sometimes reckless pioneer in art and life, between which, like Duncan, she makes no division; nor does she give one prior claim over the other. She is, Ninette de Valois believes, 'the greatest dramatic ballerina we have ever produced'.

Her dancing expresses her nature exactly; it is broad in sweep, wide in proportions, very rich in scope, where the dances do not trickle around the edges of the music, like that of so many dancers, but bear onwards in wide, sweeping phrases, in long, seemingly endless curves, as a river curves and vanishes into the distance. One is not conscious of the links between steps but only of the long flow of movement that seems to beat in waves against the music or breaks through it with an impetuous freedom.

It is interesting that Lynn Seymour possessed this open, free style from her earliest days with the Royal Ballet; although it has been enriched over the years, it has not in other ways altered. She speaks often of her stubborn nature, much apparent when she was a child and now not altogether inconspicuous, and she obviously resisted all blandishments to

*Lynn and Rudolf Nureyev: flower children.*

become a typical dancer of the English school, even when she was able to observe every day the finest example of that school, Margot Fonteyn, both in class and on the stage.

Lynn Seymour's style, while still having the flow and the sense of *plastique* of the Kirov dancers, is stronger, more physical, in many ways more elemental than theirs. It is sensual and mature, with the sensuality of a woman rather than a girl, and this has nothing to do with the dancer's own maturity, since the earthy quality of her dancing was apparent in her first roles, particularly in *The Invitation*, composed by Kenneth MacMillan in 1960, in which she created a far more realistic character than the stereotype of the violated innocent. It is that quality that made her the model for the series of dances in the style of Isadora Duncan, composed for her by Frederick Ashton in 1975/76. Both artists had the same warmth, the same sensuality and richness of movement. No other performer could cope with these dances with such conviction as Lynn Seymour; in their freedom, their innocent sensuality and their faded elegance, they belong only to Isadora Duncan and Lynn Seymour.

It is this sense of the living moment, the sensuality of the hour, that brings such extraordinary poignancy to her portrayal of Natalia Petrovna in *A Month in the Country*. Here is a young girl's love in a woman who is no longer young, who knows but cannot face the sad reality of that knowledge. We see at the same time the impetuosity of youth, only half restrained by a woman who realises, deep in her heart, that such love has no permanence and will bring her no repose.

The dancer's response to the music is also at one with her character, in the same manner as is her technique. Some very musical dancers treat the score with fastidious care: Merle Park is one of these, Margot Fonteyn was another. This is often very moving, even though it is restrained by impeccable taste. Other dancers, however, treat the music more grandly, even with a certain impatience, as if it were a waiter who is rather slow with his order; it is their servant, and must conform to their bidding. Natalia Makarova is such a dancer—imperious mistress of the score, shaping it with an imaginative daring that has a subtlety far beyond the range of the metronome. Lynn Seymour is the same kind of instinctive dancer: she does not dominate the music in quite the same manner but she is never constricted by it. In the eagerness with which she enters a dance, it seems as if she thrusts it impatiently aside, leaving it to surround the spaces she creates in movement.

It is this sense of proportioning a dance that indicates the intelligence and the imagination of Lynn Seymour's dramatic playing. Such intensity may only be maintained where the ballerina is able to develop the role continuously, so that we are able to observe the logical unfolding of character rather than a series of isolated moments which, even when they are well played, do not grow organically from those which precede them. No dramatic portrayal of hers is static; each incident holds past and future together as a whole. This is extremely difficult in ballet—far more so than in drama. Only the finest dramatic dancers can develop character like this.

The essential features of Lynn Seymour's character—

mentioned by so many people who have known her and worked with her— are all caught up and intensified in her art. It is when she is dancing that in a sense we know her best; her empathy with others, the warmth of spirit, the generosity of temperament are the human threads that make the fabric of her art. Lynn Seymour has always danced as dangerously as she has lived. She was never one of those young dancers who shiver on the edges of the music, like a bather on a cold morning. Technically she has never had the marvellous equipment of some of her contemporaries but this does not deter her, and the element of risk is never far from her dancing. Neither in art nor in life does she play safe.

It is central to our understanding of Lynn Seymour as a ballerina to appreciate the physical disadvantages that she has had to overcome. Due to the lack of intensive early training and a difficult body, she has always experienced considerable technical problems that have, by a curious paradox, shaped her art as a dramatic ballerina. She realised her weaknesses in technique in the early stages of building her career and compensated for them by a search for dramatic nuance and emotional expressiveness. Thus she began to achieve an extraordinarily liquid flow of movement, while within it each image was given its full emotional weight and colouring so that the dance became a creative act rather than a pattern of brilliantly executed academic steps. This freedom and sense of physical abandon, so much a part of Lynn Seymour's dancing, has been gained not in spite of her limitations but in a courageous defiance of them. It is this defiance that gives her art such a wide humanity, and audiences love her for this.

The dancer we see on the stage is one of us, no rare and distant being; but she is braver, more magnaminous and forgiving than most of us dare to be. 'The most painful things really do recede,' she says. 'You only remember the best.' This summarizes the truth about Lynn Seymour both as an artist and a person, framing the long perspective of the years through which this book has journeyed. Yet for an artist there is always another frontier. Like all great dancers her life is a search for a vision, at once so close that she can almost attain it, so distant she thinks it is beyond her sight. She is a pioneer, both by the inheritance of her blood and in her nature; there will always be this longing, this quest for new horizons. There are lands still unconquered, and she will find them.

# Index

224